INSIDE ISIS

INSIDE ISIS

The Brutal Rise of a Terrorist Army

BENJAMIN HALL

**CENTER
STREET**

New York Nashville Boston

6-24-16

The photos appearing on pages 10, 30, 34, 37, 40, 52, 73, 86, 100, 152, 168, 180, 218, 224, 229, and 234 are used with permission by Rick Findler.

The photos appearing on page 18, 62, and 176 are used with permission by SipaPress/REX.

The photo appearing on page 66 is used with permission by Jed Share/Getty Images.

The photo appearing on page 94 is used with permission by Jonathan Pedneault/EYE-PRESS/REX.

The photos appearing on page 120 and 138 are used with permission by REX.

The photo appearing on page 127 are used with permission by Mark Reinstien/Rex.

The photo appearing on page 128 are used with permission by AY-Collections/SipaPress/REX.

Center Street

Hachette Book Group

1290 Avenue of the Americas

New York, NY 10104

www.CenterStreet.com

Printed in the United State of America

RRD-C

Originally published in hardcover by Hachette Book Group.

First trade paperback edition: November 2015

10 9 8 7 6 5 4 3 2 1

Center Street is a division of Hachette Book Group, Inc.

The Center Street name and logo are trademarks of Hachette Book Group, Inc.

The Hachette Speakers Bureau provides a wide range of authors for speaking events. To find out more, go to www.HachetteSpeakersBureau.com or call (866) 376-6591.

The publisher is not responsible for websites (or their content) that are not owned by the publisher.

LCCN: 2015947665

ISBN 978-1-4555-9058-2 (pbk.)

One of the things that has always struck me in conflict is the amazing strength of family bonds. Even in the darkest hours, when everything else has been taken from life, there is still family, and I would like to dedicate this book to mine.

To my parents who have encouraged me despite their fears, and who have loved unconditionally. To my siblings who have taught me so much about the world. To Fatima, who always believed in me. To the love of my life, and to our new addition who's on its way; who will define me forever. I love you all.

CONTENTS

CONTENTS

INTRODUCTION

Life inside the ISIS capital of Raqqa goes on, though with a cloud hanging over it. Thousands of foreign fighters roam the streets, "morality police" patrol the neighborhoods, businesses and individuals are subjected to extortion, and women live in fear as ISIS drives them back to the Middle Ages.

Every day people are beheaded in public, stoned to death, whipped, or have their hands chopped off. They are thrown into prisons where the sound of torture is constant, and from where many people never return. Music is forbidden and prayers are forced upon the people. Gay men are thrown from roofs as punishment, babies are slaughtered in battle, all while the fighters of ISIS laugh, joke, and encourage the enslavement of girls, whom they buy, rape, and kill.

Every day that passes it becomes harder to shake them from their hives. The longer we allow them to consolidate gains, the longer they have to persuade people that there is no alternative.

A new generation of children will grow up knowing

nothing but contempt and blood lust toward us. Already they want to carry guns, they tell on their own parents, and they are forbidden any education other than the Koran. If we allow these children to be brainwashed, it will lead us toward a clash of civilizations and the end of any reformation—this is exactly what ISIS wants.

No, we must be proactive, we must root them out, and we must not give them the semblance of a state—they are not a state, they are terrorists. They are fanatics, and there's no room for them in today's world.

ISIS is intent on our destruction—there is no doubt about that—their beliefs are in direct contrast to ours, and they will continue attacking us as long as they breathe.

Even though the administration claims they're not gaining more ground, the situation is getting worse. They are increasing their hold in the cities, tightening control on the areas they rule, encouraging people to strike at us, and still murdering and torturing thousands of innocent people. We must not allow a fanatic state to grow strong in the center of Syria and Iraq, we must not allow these people—who are set on our destruction—to create a base from where they can attack us, and above all, we must not kowtow to others in our attempts to prevent this.

It's almost impossible to gauge their true numbers, but in December 2014, the CIA believed that ISIS could "muster between 20,000 and 31,500 fighters" between Iraq and Syria, and their ranks continue to swell as extremists flock from around the world.

I'll never forget the first time I faced ISIS; the first time I saw their black flags fluttering in the dry heat, and the first time I saw their men pacing up and down, just fifty meters away; laughing, playing, and goading us. There they were, on the other side of a bridge, a bridge that marked the front line between us and them, which marked the unfathomable gap between right and wrong, good and evil.

There was confidence in their steps, and I could hear them laughing. They brandished their weapons, put their arms around each other, and waved at us. They were better armed, better prepared, and better funded than the soldiers we were with, and they knew it.

They were eager to fight, hoping to die, and they hid behind nothing, while at the same time the company of Kurdish troops which was crouched beside me, hid low behind sand banks; peeking out, hoping for the best, and praying to be saved.

It was this confidence that really struck me, and which they exhibit to this day. Their soldiers, versus those they face, are so full of zeal, so eager to kill, so sure of themselves, that it's put fear into the hearts of their enemies. It's their sheer belief that is so terrifying to others. But despite their brutality and strength, they can be beaten.

Photographer Rick Findler and I have covered conflicts in the region for six years, moving, as others have, from conflict to conflict, watching revolutions intended to usher in freedom, be hijacked, as a far greater evil takes hold.

I remember the sheer joy of fighters in Libya, as they freed their cities and reclaimed their country—prisoners being freed and families reunited. I remember the early days of the Syrian revolution, when people believed they were shaking off their dictator, and cheered in the streets; and in Egypt, where Tahrir square symbolized a new democracy, one which would define the region. But today all that hope has gone—and the Middle East is faced with a greater enemy than before, one intent on spreading its web, and which is doing so successfully.

The story of ISIS is not just about vicious jihadis, or about Syria or Iraq or the Middle East. It's about a whole generation of chaos, a whole region in turmoil, and a whole world at threat. It is a problem that will define the Middle East, and in turn the West, for decades, and it is one that must be addressed now. This book will take you behind the scenes, inside their cities, training camps, and prisons. It will recount the battles which defined their rise, the recruitment process, the propaganda arm, the money, and the politics. It will take you inside their world.

In many respects this chaos was inevitable; so many different groups and countries in the region had their own agendas, and so many were intent on the destruction of others for religious and political reasons. Yet these internal divisions also create hatred toward the West, and are something we must deal with—that we should have been dealing with. But things have then been made worse, by the apparent apathy of the Obama administration. Obama's policy of strategic disengagement has led the Middle East to a tipping point, and unless something is done soon, this threat will define a generation—it may be too late. So many opportunities have been missed, yet we must act now. This is Al-Qaeda 2.0; more powerful and more brutal.

It is quite simply mind-boggling that the conditions ISIS needed to thrive, occurred at precisely the right time, in precisely the right place, aligning all the stars. And what it has grown into is not just an army that can be defeated on the battlefield, it is an ideology, and one that grows stronger by the day. It is a result of everything that has happened in the Middle East over the last century, and one that may well dominate for a century to come.

It is said that ISIS achieved in two years what Al-Qaeda could not do in twenty, controlling large swathes of land across Iraq and Syria. But unlike Al-Qaeda, ISIS is not hidden high in mountain caves; it is standing proudly on the plains of Nineveh, well armed, well funded, and crying out for battle. Nor is it an exaggeration to imagine that ISIS will have a base in the region for years to come; the grip they have on local populations amid the chaos of the Syrian conflict, the very sectarian nature of the war, the vast funds they now control, and the actions of the puppet masters fueling them, means weeding out this cancer will be immensely hard to do.

ISIS now poses a threat, not only to regional stability, but potentially to world order. The idea that we can contain chaos in the Middle East without it escalating is untrue, and without Western action so far, they would surely be controlling much more territory than they do. Their rapid rise to power and their continuing ability to confound even the United States, combined with all the factors in their favor, has laid the conditions for what is a perfect storm.

The rise of ISIS must also be seen within the context of a proxy war between Saudi Arabia and Iran. It is an age-old battle for regional influence and ultimate domination of the other. Much as the Cold War between the United States and Russia escalated, so too is this one between Sunni and Shia masters, both intent on the other's destruction.

But this is also a tale of great sadness, and the human consequences are simply devastating. Caught amid the battles and the politics are millions of people who have lost everything. Families torn apart, civilizations destroyed, and whole cultures razed to the ground. The great tragedy is that for so many people, this is merely a game of chess.

The rise of the Arab Spring brought with it such hope that the overthrow of dictators would usher in new democracies, new freedoms, and new Western-friendly governments. But this simply was not to be. Too many countries were shorn in two, having lived too long under oppression, and forgiving sins of the past became impossible. The crucial example now is Bashar al-Assad, who by holding on to power, by stoking sectarian flames, is creating the perfect conditions for ISIS to thrive.

When we look at the origins of ISIS, it is a tale of new names, old names, of morphing identities, and twisting allegiances. They sprung out of nowhere, and in a matter of just two years have claimed to have established their caliphate.

For anyone who thinks these people are just raving mad terrorists, think again. They are immensely driven, incredibly organized, and adaptable, and will not think twice about committing genocide or ethnic cleansing. They are a threat that must be taken seriously.

ISIS has been called numerous names since its inception in 2013. ISIS, ISIL, IS, and DAESH. But what's in a name? Which is correct? To clear up any confusion I want to explain what each means, and why I've chosen to call them ISIS.

The first name we knew them by was ISIS; an acronym for "The Islamic State in Iraq and Al-Sham"—a literal translation of their Arabic name "Al-Dawla Al-Islamiya fi al-Iraq wa al-Sham." Al Sham is the wider region of Syria—an area that includes Syria, Lebanon, parts of Turkey and Jordan. It is the historical Islamic province of the region as drawn up following the Muslim conquest of Syria in the seventh century.

Previously ISIS had just been ISI (Islamic state in Iraq) and by adding al-Sham to this, they quickly set their sights on conquering the rest of the region, and expanding.

The other name we know them by is ISIL, you will hear President Obama using this term. Effectively it's the same as ISIS, except the L refers to 'The Levant' rather than "Al-Sham" The Levant is the same area as Al-Sham, but is the English word for it—it's a bit outdated now. It's taken from the Latin word "Levare" which means to rise, and refers to the lands over which the sun rose across the Mediterranean during the Roman empire. This is Syria, Lebanon, Turkey, Jordan and also includes parts of Egypt.

In June 2014 ISIS announced they would be changing their name to 'The Islamic State'. Amazingly much of the mainstream media followed suit, using the name the terrorist had picked themselves. Herein lies a great problem. By declaring that they were the "Islamic State" they sought to legitimize themselves—claiming ownership over the Caliphate, and declaring themselves a independent nation.

Not only is it ridiculous to allow a group of terrorists to decide their own name, but even more absurd to happily accept their announcement of statehood. Even the majority of Muslims around the world objected to this arrogance, yet the Media continues to use it.

Finally there is DAESH, which is the acronym you get if you use the first letter of the Arabic meaning. This is the widely use term in the Middle East, and although it's an acronym of their official name, it is also terribly derogatory; and the ISIS members can't stand it. That's because the alternative reading of the word Daesh means they are trampled under foot, and crushed in the dust. It's a word that, which if it had more recognition I would happily have used myself.

But for the purpose of the book we will go with the name they first came to be known as: ISIS.

INSIDE ISIS

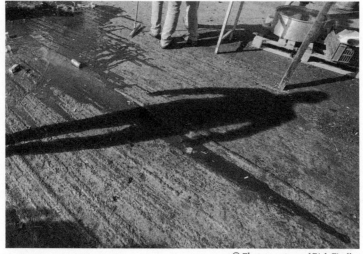

The shadow of a bomb squad member falls over a stream of blood.
Baghdad, Iraq—December 2013.

CHAPTER ONE

ISIS Homecoming

Baghdad, Iraq, November 2013

The pilgrims walked slowly toward Karbala in the brisk morning air of the Iraqi winter. Men, women, and children shuffled along the crowded road, some praying, some waving banners, all tired.

The mood was jubilant for this was Ashura, the most important Shia pilgrimage of the year, and approximately fifteen million people were journeying to the holy shrine of Imam Hussein, to celebrate his martyrdom.

The highway had been closed between Baghdad and Karbala, and the whole length was lined with tents, offering rest and food for the pilgrims. People mingled inside, shared their food, and ate from large communal cauldrons filled with rice, meat, and vegetables, which had been supplied by the government. Families were celebrating.

It was into one of these tents that the suicide bomber walked. Avoiding the numerous security cordons along the way, he had found his way inside, intent on killing his Shia enemy.

Throwing his arms to the air, he cried out, "*Allahu Akbar*" (God is greater) before reaching down to detonate his vest. Soldiers nearby pounced on him, pinning his arms to his side, struggling to secure them. As the commotion grew and people panicked, he pushed away, freed one of his hands, and detonated.

The blast ripped through the tent, evaporating those nearest to him, and sent body parts up to 650 feet through the air. Ten people died instantaneously, among them two children, and thirty-four others were wounded.

There is nothing quite so sickening as the scene of a bomb blast. The rivers of blood cover the road, and body pieces lie everywhere: on walls, on cars, and on people. Arms, torsos, matted hair, and toes are everywhere. The wounded are rushed away however they can be carried. Men walk around filling garbage bags with body parts, picking up toes and hands, then taking the bags, dripping with blood and fat, into a van so relatives have something to bury.

Hundreds of police and soldiers from different units mill around: arguing, shouting, and fighting over jurisdiction. It's chaotic. Family members and friends trample over the scene wailing, leading to even more disputes, and very quickly riots erupt. As a Westerner the blame often falls on you: "Spies, Israeli spies!" people shout.

Bombs are just a part of life in Iraq. They're hidden in pens, torches, books, tea cups, and flagpoles;

in discarded phone chargers and in shoes—anything that children or others might pick up and take home. Such is the indiscriminate nature of the attacks. It's this brutality that has defined the rise of ISIS, and while one can argue forever about who first escalated the sectarianism, today each side blames the other, and each side is to blame.

Maliki Does Wrong

"The coaching, and teaching, and mentoring, the thousands of interactions at the local level were all wasted by the government of Iraq that chose deliberately to follow a sectarian agenda and alienate entire segments of the population, which created an environment in which ISIS could return and could flourish"
—General Dempsey

Despite popular belief that ISIS grew out of the Syrian revolution, it was actually in Iraq that it was born and grew strong. It was the decade of suicide attacks by terrorists on one side and sectarian brutality from the government on the other that led Iraq to the brink. Daily attacks on both sides led to the conditions that allowed ISIS to thrive.

Yes, it was in Syria that ISIS became the power it is today, hidden among the splintered, chaotic battleground, but it was in Iraq where the seeds were first sown, and where sectarian discontent created the conditions that allowed them to prosper. It was during the years following the US led invasion of 2003, and the subsequent attempts to rebuild the shattered nation, that we saw a black cloud developing.

After defeating Saddam's army, the first thing the United States did was to create a new inclusive government, one that would take into account the sectarian divisions within the country. The prime minister would be Shia, the president would be Kurdish, and the deputy prime minister would be Sunni. However this soon failed, and President Nouri al-Maliki began to consolidate power around him, ignoring pleas for him not to. He created a politicized security apparatus answerable only to him, and he looked to his neighbor Shia Iran for guidance and support. As General Dempsey, chairman of the Joint Chiefs of Staff said, "We gave Iraq a chance—an opportunity. They failed to take that opportunity."

Iran had fought a decades long battle against Saddam Hussein, from 1980 to 1988, so when he was deposed in 2003, Tehran was determined to replace the enemy on their border with an ally. Controlling Iraq would also give them a direct passage to their allies and proxies in Syria and Lebanon, and allow them to project influence against their archenemies Saudi Arabia and Israel.

And so Iran began helping Maliki tighten his grip on the country by isolating Sunni regions in the west, and crushing Kurdish dreams of independence in the north. As Iran grew stronger in Iraq, Maliki began answering directly to Tehran. It's a great irony that Iran, America's great enemy, benefited most from the US war in Iraq.

The principal error made in the postwar years was

the immediate banning of all members of Saddam's Ba'athist party. No former Ba'athists were allowed to join the newly established Iraqi army (a huge part of the country's work and security force), and as a result the country was left in the hands of people with little experience, while many disgruntled Ba'athists lost everything. Thousands were left jobless: teachers, doctors, professors, and soldiers were all banned from holding public sector positions because they had joined Saddam's party—which had been practically imperative under his regime.

They found themselves unable to support and feed their families, and their anger grew to the point that joining Sunni terrorist movements in the west of the country seemed to be the only alternative—the only way to change their downfall. This purge of Ba'athists is considered one of the major blunders of the invasion; it removed all experienced officers from the pool of candidates, leaving only inexperienced soldiers to run the newly formed defense forces, and although it was partly overturned in 2008, the damage had been done: Maliki's Shia had control, and they were not going to cede it.

Nostalgia

"Here's the Saddamists who are assisting ISIS, who started the insurgency after Saddam was deposed as a regime, they started the insurgency with money, significant amounts of human capital, significant amount of weapons and ammunition, etc. It was probably the most solvent insurgency in the history of modern times."

   —General Keane,
      Former Deputy Chief of Staff,
      United States Army

During these postwar years, many Sunnis across western Iraq also grew nostalgic for the security of Saddam's era—a time when, despite the authoritarian rules, they had been closer to power and not indiscriminately bombed and attacked on a daily basis. His image started to become popular again in the north and west of Iraq, and his picture could be found hanging in many houses. Iraqi soldiers I embedded with in 2012 would unashamedly called out, "Father, father," while they watched video tributes to him and his sons.

Saddam's daughter Raghad Hussein, who now lives in Jordan, also gave an interview after the ISIS attack on Mosul voicing her support. "I am happy to see all these victories," she said. "Someday, I will return to Iraq and visit my father's grave. Maybe it won't happen very soon, but it will certainly happen." She has since been indicted by Interpol, for "inciting terrorism in Iraq."

For ten long years, members of the Ba'athist party

hid in the shadows of Iraq, dreaming of the day they would take back the country. They lay low in their Sunni communities, gaining ever more support as a result of the attacks by the central government—they were regularly detained and tortured, and would disappear. Ultimately, it was the failure of the US government to include these elements in post-Saddam Iraq that created the conditions for ISIS to thrive, and it is one that came to define the current storm.

Tapping into strong tribal ties in the region and the vast military experience among them, these ex-Ba'athists were able to command countless followers, while also exerting influence over ISIS. The top three ISIS generals in the takeover of Mosul were Ba'athists, as were eight of the top ten in ISIS at the time. Izzat Ibrahim al-Douri, a former military commander whom Saddam considered to be like a brother, was widely rumored to be in Mosul overseeing the conflict, after hiding out in Qatar and Syria for a decade—he is still a leading figure in ISIS.

As ISIS pushed through Iraq in June 2014, it was this network that helped it control the villages and towns it captured along the way. The core army of terrorists and freed soldiers could continue moving forward toward others targets: Baghdad and the holy Shia cities of Karbala and Najaf, while the favorable, disenfranchised Sunni tribes kept control. "As an effective fighting force alone, ISIS would never have been able to hold such large territories," a Kurdish intelligence officer told me, "but with the help of Ba'athists and Sunni tribes (united under the new name the Naqshbandi Army), they have been able to keep the momentum going."

It will be the reversal of these allegiances that will be crucial in stopping ISIS, for ultimately many ISIS allies in Iraq are nationalists, rather than jihadis, who chose to pick what they saw as the lesser of two evils—and there is precedence for such a reversal.

Pre-ISIS Years

Abu Musab al-Zarqawi, leader of Al-Qaeda in Iraq (AQI) until his death in 2006. With a twenty-five million dollar bounty on his head, he was considered the greatest sole threat to US troops post invasion.

ISIS certainly didn't grow strong exclusively as a result of ex-Ba'athists and disgruntled Sunni tribesmen. While this is indeed what gave them their early power in Iraq, their radical core has had a presence in the country for decades, and they have a fine pedigree as far as global jihad is concerned. It is directly from these groups that ISIS was born.

In 1999, a terrorist group named Jama'at al-Tawhid wal-Jihad (Tawhid literally means the Unity and Jihad group) came to prominence in the western Sunni region of Anbar. Tawhid had been founded in Jordan in the 1990s by the infamous Abu Musab al-Zarqawi, one of the many fighters who had fought against the Russians in Afghanistan.

Upon his return to Jordan, Zarqawi was arrested and sentenced to six years in prison for possessing guns and explosives. Upon his release in 1999, having attempted to blow up the Radisson Hotel in Amman, he fled to the Pakistan/Afghanistan border, where he set up training camps with the help of a two hundred thousand dollar investment from his old friend Osama bin Laden, whom he had known from his Afghanistan days. After fighting against the United States in Afghanistan until 2001, he eventually moved his group to Iraq having allegedly received safekeeping and support from an unlikely patron—Iran.

Shia Iran has been known to fund Sunni extremists throughout the region, despite their deep-seated hatred of each other. Initially this was to destabilize Saddam's regime and counter Saudi hegemony. It's known that many jihadi fighters have used the mountainous region between Iraq and Iran as a safe haven, and in 2000, Iran refused Jordanian extradition requests for Zarqawi, who had by now been sentenced to death. This balancing act played by Iran is a major factor in the ISIS story, and we see them supporting a number of various groups to use as tools in their own geopolitical game—including many of the elements that precede ISIS.

In 2004, following a number of major successful attacks in Iraq against US troops, Zarqawi swore allegiance to Bin Laden, and Tawhid morphed into Al-Qaeda in Iraq (AQI)—a group whose full name is Tanzim Qaidat al-Jihad fi Bilad al-Rafidayn, literally meaning the Organization of Jihad's base in the country of the two rivers. These attacks were both brutal and indiscriminate. Zarqawi is known to have used the mentally disabled as suicide bombers, to have hidden bombs inside coffins to target funerals, and to have personally decapitated the Western hostages Nick Berg and Eugene Armstrong.

Rising up against the United States-led invasion, and with much support among Sunni tribes who resisted occupation, foreign fighters from the region flocked to AQI to do battle with the United States, wreaking havoc throughout the supposed fledgling democracy. In the same way that US involvement today acts as a catalyst to recruit jihadists, it did so as well back then, leading to a war many saw as battling the crusading invaders.

By 2005, AQI was a potent force in Iraq, and Zarqawi was the most wanted man with a twenty-five million dollar bounty on his head. Seeking to grow, he merged with the Mujahideen Shura Council (MSC), a network of other jihadi groups, and the newly founded army became the Islamic State in Iraq (ISI)—the direct precursor to ISIS. ISI fought a brutal war against the United States, using many of the same tactics seen today, but in 2005, local sheiks who had become sickened by their brutality, and upset at their attempts to control their illicit businesses (principally oil and gas smuggling), founded a group called the Sons of Iraq to counter them.

Sunni Awakening

It was the Sons of Iraq who ultimately rose up and defeated ISI in Iraq with extensive support from the United States, who began paying their salaries and providing logistical support and weapons. In 2006, Zarqawi was killed by a United States bomb strike, and in 2008, the Sons of Iraq and local "Awakening Councils" had effectively thrown out ISI in what was one of the great stories of the war and of United States-Iraqi cooperation. The United States hopes to use this same model against ISIS in western Iraq, and these same Sunni tribes are being encouraged to help overthrow ISIS.

At their peak, the Sons of Iraq numbered fifty-four thousand Sunni fighters, who had come together to successfully defeat ISI, but when in 2008 the United States ceded responsibility for their salaries to the central government in Baghdad, it fell apart. The Maliki central government—terrified of an armed Sunni movement in the west—rejected the possibility of them becoming a permanent military force. The Maliki government stopped paying their salaries and began detaining people, torturing them, and holding them in secret prisons. Some disappeared forever.

But the downfall came when Obama was sworn in—his immediate strategy was to disengage from the Middle East and pull out of Iraq, just as they were getting back on their feet. He failed to push through the Status of Forces agreement which would have seen some US troops stay in the country, and this led to the security breakdown.

I spoke to General Jack Keane, retired four-star general and one of the architects of the United States surge in 2009. He explained the situation. "In 2009, violence in Iraq had gone down ninety percent and Al-Qaeda at the time had been defeated. I saw the messages; we captured signals and email traffic that they were transmitting to Al-Qaeda central in Pakistan saying 'don't send anymore foreign fighters. This war is over. We are defeated here.'"

"The problem was, we had this nefarious character Maliki. I believe that pulling away from Maliki as Obama did, and leaving him to his own devices just inflamed his own paranoia and insecurity. So here comes Obama who made up his mind to do two things—get out of Iraq and get out of Afghanistan as quickly as possible, and in doing so, plays right into the Iranians hands. Iran's leaders must have said, "This guy Obama is walking away from Iraq, can you believe it, and he's opening the door for us!"

"Maliki wanted to remain a strong ally to the United States, he had made the decision, he wanted a long term strategic relationship with the United States, but Obama pulled away from all of that."

In July 2010, the growing remnants of ISI were taken over by Abu Bakr Baghdadi—the self-proclaimed Caliph and brutal leader of ISIS. The stage was set.

CHAPTER TWO

The Caliph

Cold, calculating, and a master of disguise, Abu Bakr Baghdadi emerged from obscurity to take over the reins of ISI. Born Ibrahim Awwad Ibrahim Ali al-Badri al-Samarrai in 1971 in Samarra, a town north of Baghdad; his parents were preachers, and he set off down the same path. At age eighteen, he attended the Islamic University of Baghdad, where he spent the next ten years studying. ISIS propaganda claims he received a BA, an MA, and a PhD in sharia law, but this cannot be verified.

People in the district of Tobchi, where he lived while at the University, remember him as a quiet and retiring person who excelled only at football. He occasionally led prayers in the local mosque, but according to those who he knew, he was never an imam—again as ISIS claims.

Baghdadi married and had a son. In 1999, a few years after he finished his studies, US intelligence reports claim he had become Al-Qaeda's man in Al-Qa'im, a small town in Iraq's vast western Anbar province on the border of Syria. A Pentagon document from 2005 says that while there, under the nom de guerre Abu Duaa, "he was connected to the intimidation, torture, and murder of local civilians. He would kidnap individuals or entire families, accuse them, pronounce sentence, and publicly execute them."

The difficulty here is that nom de guerres are widely used, and although this brutal character would fit with the style of ISIS leadership today, it's not certain that this "Abu Duaa" was Baghdadi. As Lieutenant-General Sir Graeme Lamb, a British special forces commander at the time says, "We either arrested or killed a man of that name about half a dozen times, he is like a wraith who keeps reappearing, and I am not sure where fact and fiction meet."

Rewards for Justice
Stop a terrorist. Save lives.

WANTED

Information that brings to justice...

Abu Du'a
Up to $10 Million Reward

Abu Du'a, also known as Abu Bakr al-Baghdadi, is the senior leader of the terrorist organization, the Islamic State of Iraq and the Levant (ISIL). Reflecting its greater regional ambitions, al-Qaida in Iraq changed its name in 2013 to ISIL and stepped up its attacks across Syria and Iraq. ISIL attacks are calculated, coordinated, and part of a strategic campaign. Abu Du'a is in charge of overseeing all operations and is currently based in Syria.

Abu Du'a has taken personal credit for a series of terrorist attacks in Iraq since 2011 and claimed credit for the June 2013 operations against the Abu Ghraib prison outside Baghdad, the March 2013 suicide bombing assault on the Ministry of Justice, among other attacks against Iraqi Security Forces and Iraqi citizens going about their daily lives.

Abu Du'a is a Specially Designated Global Terrorist under Executive Order 13224. He is also listed at the United Nations Security Council 1267/1989 al-Qaida Sanctions Committee.

Date of Birth: 1971	**Submit a Tip**
	www.rewardsforjustice.net
Place of Birth: Samarra, Iraq	1-800-US-REWARD
	(1-800-877-3927)
Hair: Black	RFJ@state.gov
Eyes: Brown	
Sex: Male	
Complexion: Olive	
Aliases: Dr. Ibrahim 'Awwad Ibrahim 'Ali al-Badri al-Samarrai', Ibrahim 'Awad Ibrahim al-Badri al Samarrai, Abu Duaa', Dr. Ibrahim, Abu Bakr al-Baghdadi	

Wanted: US State Department poster, for Abu Bakr al-Baghdadi, founder of ISIS.

Sources within ISIS claim he uses body doubles,

never meets with his face uncovered, and is known to very few.

Camp Bucca

In late 2005, Baghdadi was arrested by the United States as a known Al-Qaeda affiliate. He was placed in Camp Bucca where he met many of the people who would go on to found ISIS with him later, and where his beliefs were certainly compounded. Camp Bucca was the largest detention center in the country under the United States occupation, housing around twenty-four thousand detainees at any one time, and some former prisoners have said that it was effectively a "terrorists training facility," and that lessons were taught on how to commit terrorist attacks, and those adopting western ways were savagely beaten.

Bucca was a sprawling campus of barbed wire, tents, and countless compounds. Guards, many of them reservists, had to deal with sandstorms, 140 degree days, and freezing cold nights.

In total, nine senior ISIS leaders are known to have spent time with Baghdadi in Camp Bucca; among them his deputy, a former Lieutenant Colonel in Saddam's army, and the men in charge of ISIS foreign fighters, suicide bombers, warehouses, and orphans.

There is a good chance that some of these men crossed paths with Baghdadi while there. He was never placed in the secure unit Compound Fourteen, as he was not considered a grave threat, and indeed an officer at the camp, Colonel Kenneth King, remembers him as a quieter inmate. It seems very likely that radicals and

Ba'athists mingled and plotted while wiling away the time.

If not plotting, the detainees were fighting. The guards came under regular attack from homemade weapons—knives, machetes, whips and nunchucks were often found in the rooms. Detainees dug tunnels throughout the camp, tore up tents to make fake army uniforms, and on a number of occasions successfully escaped, though they were almost always picked up in the surrounding deserts.

One of the more inventive weapons—and one of the favorites—was nicknamed "Chai Rocks." Detainees would blend their tea (chai) with dirt and make rocks, which they then let harden in the sun. These rocks would then be fired at guards using slingshots of any kind—causing serious harm.

Riots often broke out, though usually they were aimed at opposing inmates, not at guards, and because of this, detainees from different religions, tribes, or sects were eventually segregated. Disputes among the prisoners tended to be resolved through their own sharia courts, and those found guilty of "Western behavior" could be severely punished. One man who had been accused of helping the United States was attacked by other inmates and had his eyes gouged out.

Guards became adept at identifying the extremists and leaders by their interactions with others, though none of the guards remember Baghdadi as a trouble-maker. Eventually, as the growing extremist threat grew, they began bringing in clerics to teach a more moderate version of the Koran, and attempted to offer anti-radicalization classes. The problem was, if a detainee attended them, they risked being accused of collusion.

Baghdadi was released from Bucca in September 2009, when control was handed over to the Iraqi Army, possibly as part of an amnesty by the Iraqi government, but possibly because Baghdadi had successfully stayed below the radar. According to the camp commander at the time, his last words were, "See you in NY."

Baghdadi Grows Strong

In July 2010, having been released from Camp Bucca, Baghdadi was appointed leader of the resurgent ISI following the death of his predecessor, Abu Omar al-Baghdadi. He was voted in by nine of the eleven Shura council members, and announced the head of Al-Qaeda in Iraq. That he rose so quickly following his release from Bucca, having received such great support, suggests he had been quietly cultivating allies inside the camp.

For the next few years, he masterminded several large-scale attacks in Baghdad, which targeted Sunni lawmakers and Shias alike. It seems that from early on, he sought to stoke sectarian flames. Three days after the death of bin Laden, Baghdadi vowed retaliation for his death. In a statement he released eulogizing the leader, he claimed he would unleash one hundred strikes. Between March and April 2011, Baghdadi successfully launched twenty-three attacks in a brutal spree, killing hundreds—The first of many coordinated attacks.

Although Baghdadi swore allegiance to Ayman al-Zawhiri, bin Laden's successor, he also started to grow a following of his own, and he consolidated his own position. He began to bolster the group's leadership with disenfranchised Ba'athist and Saddam-era commanders, and he announced publicly that he would be returning to the former strongholds from where they had been driven by the Americans. He was true to his word.

Jailbreak

On July 21, 2012, Baghdadi announced the start of a campaign called "Breaking the Walls." It was his plan to "refuel" the group and free jihadi prisoners around the country, and it would last exactly one year. What ensued was a sequence of well-orchestrated and violent attacks on prisons holding the worst offenders from around the country. At the same time, he increased targeted assassinations and continued to stoke sectarian differences, which he knew would be key to his future take-over of Anbar province. His decision to announce the plan beforehand was the first sign of what would become an ISIS military trademark: dictating the terms of warfare. "Breaking the Walls" showed Baghdadi's ability to plan, finance, supply, and carry out multiple coordinated raids at the same time, and in doing this, he wreaked havoc around the country.

Over the next year, eight prisons were hit, and Vehicle-Borne Improvised Explosive Device (VBIED) attacks escalated dramatically around the country, leading to the final attack on the infamous Abu Ghraib prison, west of Baghdad. Baghdadi launched diversionary attacks in the days preceding the final attack, including eight simultaneous VBEID attacks around Baghdad. Not only did he attack the prison itself, but at the same time attacked military installations in the area.

At nine thirty in the evening on Sunday, July 21, 2013, the attack began. Multiple VBIEDs, suicide bombers, and rocket-propelled grenades were unleashed on the hardened outside perimeter, as his forces began their assault. Once the walls and fences were breached, ISI fighters swarmed into the darkened compound. There was a vicious battle for a couple of hours, until finally the compound was overrun; over five hundred prisoners were freed.

It's not easy to quickly hide five hundred prisoners in an area controlled by an enemy army, but Baghdadi had planned their escape as well. As continued attacks around Baghdad diverted forces, the prisoners escaped by foot, fleeing in all directions from the prison. They headed to various meeting points in the surrounding countryside, where convoys of cars were waiting to ferry them away. The convicts quickly accessed the ring road system around Baghdad from where they could flee to their various hideouts within old Al-Qaeda safe havens in the surrounding villages. It seems clear that they were prepped beforehand, and reports indicate that each man knew where to go.

These prisoners were the worst of the worst—the ones the US had been mopping up between 2006 and 2008. But suddenly they were free, and answerable to Baghdadi and ISI. He had his army, and it wouldn't be too long before ISIS was born, for across the border in Syria, the conflict was raging.

© Photo courtesy of Rick Findler

A demolished mosque in Azaz, northern Syria—October, 2012.

CHAPTER THREE

Syria's Collapse

"The reality is that defeating Islamic State also requires defeating Bashar Assad. Avoiding this reality, as Mr. Obama still tries to do, will only postpone the problem at growing risk to Syrian lives and American security. And when Syria deteriorates further, as it surely will, the U.S. will be compelled to respond once again, but our options will be fewer, worse and costlier."

—Senator John McCain and
   Senator Lyndsey Graham

Idlib, Syria 2012

Headlights from a column of Syrian military vehicles could be seen far below us, snaking their way slowly toward the cave. As we sat huddled around the makeshift stove that had given us warmth for the previous few days, members of the Free Syrian Army argued around us. The question they were debating was whether to turn us over to the regime, or fight to save us. We had no input as our fate was being decided.

Abu Ali, the commander, was adamant that he smuggle us back to Turkey. He believed we had to tell the world what we had seen, but his men knew that it meant added brutality toward them and their families. It was ultimately because of us that the trucks were coming, and the situation was tense.

The day before, photographer Rick Findler and I had been smuggled into the crowded streets of Taftanaz, a poor farming village thirty miles inside Syria. Members of the Free Syrian Army—local men who had joined the fight against Bashar al-Assad to protect their families—had been showing us the devastation wreaked by government forces. The conflict had been going for only a few months, and yet in that short time, it had already escalated. That evening at dusk, a peaceful protest was happening as the people mourned new deaths. Earlier that day, a small enclave of houses nearby had been attacked by Syrian troops for no reason other than to warn people against rising up.

The village had not just been destroyed. It had been shelled, dynamited, and finally bulldozed, leaving nothing more than blocks of rubble for streets and streets. In the troops' wake, Shabiha death squads had ridden through the town firing openly from the windows at passersby, mowing them down. It was for this reason that the people had gathered that night, to protest against the regime.

As the children around us that day led the chants, gunfire suddenly erupted from the rooftops. Assad's forces had crept around and opened fire into the innocent crowds. It was chaos, and we were quickly ushered away. Many locals turned on us too, screaming and lashing out, fearing that our presence there would only make things worse for them—they were afraid of everything.

Later that day, as we hid in the cave, we heard that the army knew we had filmed the attack and that they were coming to find us. It was for this reason that we found our fate the subject of an angry debate. There were middlemen in the region, people that acted as go-betweens, talking to both the regime and the rebels, and they had let it be known that the army wanted us handed over.

After two hours of debate, Abu Ali won, and we were quickly bundled over the hills on bikes, then from car to car toward the border. Another regime offensive was happening to the north of us, so counter-intuitively, in order for us to escape, we had to drive deeper in to Syria, deeper into Assad territory before flanking them. As we approached a small village, armed men jumped in to the road ahead of us, screaming. Bullets flew past the car, and the two fighters in the front reached for their guns.

Screaming at them not to fight, our fixer ushered us out of the car, our hands raised high—another bullet raced past. Our hearts raced as they approached us. Then one of them recognized us. Both groups had thought the other were Shabiha militia, who were in pursuit just a mile behind us. When we got away from the front, having clambered a mile over steep rocks back to the Turkish border it was like being given a new lease on life.

Syria

© Photo courtesy of Rick Findler

Refugees flee the fighting in Northern Syria—May 2012.

The Syrian conflict is one of recent history's great tragedies, not least because the country appeared to be progressing before it descended into chaos. Assad had made the right noises about opening up his country, released hundreds of political prisoners arrested by his father, encouraged some political dialogue, and married into a Sunni family. Westerners flocked to the beautiful bazaars of Aleppo and the souk in Damascus, and returned with stories of the kindness of the Syrian people and their warm hospitality.

But today, the bazaars are destroyed, and the majority of Syrians have been displaced. How did it go so wrong?

Early on in the War on Terror—2001 onwards—Syria had been an unofficial partner of the United States, as had Iran, sharing intel against threats. In 2007, the

United States asked for Assad's help to fight the radicals in western Iraq; principally Al-Qaeda in Iraq, which Baghdadi would eventually take over. Syria had interrogated militants at the behest of the United States.

However, at the same time, Syria played both sides by giving safe passage to, and harboring, many of the same terrorists they were fighting, as well as Hamas and Hezbollah, whom they hoped would destabilize Iraq and complicate United States strategy.

After the overthrow of Saddam in 2003, Syria's support for these groups became too much for the United States, and by 2010 Syria had become a strong piece in what President Bush called the Axis of Evil. So when the revolution started in 2012, many people hoped and believed that it would follow the path of Tunisia, Egypt, and Libya; countries that had initially thrown off their oppressive regimes and appeared to be moving toward democracy. We now know this to be false, as Egypt has reverted to military rule, and Libya has crumbled. At the time, there was great hope that the region would go through its own reformation.

But it was not to be, and history repeated itself. Time and time again, revolutions have been hijacked by powers lurking in the shadows, rather than won by those who rise up, and the removal of strong leaders, has more often than not, led to huge periods of instability. As with Muammar Qaddafi, Saddam Hussein, Hosni Mubarak, and now Bashar Assad, countries once held together by brutality erupted along sectarian lines.

Following the arrest of fifteen teenagers who had been caught daubing anti-Assad phrases on a wall in Daraa, and the subsequent killing of 120 protesters, Syrians began to rise up. This was the spark that set off the fire.

Soon, hundreds of people were protesting peacefully on the streets, demanding the teenagers' release. Assad, terrified of being the next leader to fall, was unwilling to relinquish power, and buoyed by the support of Iran and Russia, he embarked on a heavy-handed tactic of fear, seeking to beat the local people into submission.

His father had successfully done the same in 1980, with the massacre of twenty thousand people in Hama following an assassination attempt by the Muslim Brotherhood. And young Bashar tried again. Rather than agree to concessions laid out before him, he turned his vastly superior armed forces against the innocent population and began destroying whole villages in the areas that rose up.

Early on, his army stayed secure in its bases, leaving them only in heavily armored convoys to attack at random. He wanted to demonstrate to the people that they couldn't win, that they had no chance of winning—and in those early days he was right. I remember being there as the revolution began, hiding in the mountain caves with rebels, and seeing people throw their arms in the air, and kneel submissively in the streets. "What can we do?" They all cried. "Help us."

At that stage, the extent of the resistance was a small guerrilla war fought with hunting rifles and a few old Kalashnikovs, coupled with peaceful protests in the streets. Moving around the countryside meant exploding homemade pipe bombs on one road to divert attention away from another, or using generations-old paths that only locals knew to move through the hills.

But despite Assad's attempts to crack down, the people would not give up. They had watched the Arab Spring unfold, and were ready for their turn. It has to be said that at this point it was a pure nascent rebel movement, one of people rising up against their dictator.

But whether it was weariness from the decade of conflict in the Middle East, or the lack of a viable solution, nothing was done to help them. Intelligence reports suggesting Syria would become a breeding ground for terrorists were swept under the rug, and although Obama had been briefed on numerous occasions about the rise of ISIS, he chose to ignore it.

Assad

© Photo courtesy of Rick Findler

Rebels fighters show their hatred for President Bashar al Assad. Aleppo, Syria—January 2013.

Assad had never expected to become a leader; it was his elder brother Basil who was the heir apparent. However, Basil died in a car crash on his way to Damascus airport in 1994, and Bashar, who at the time was doing a residency in ophthalmology in London, was propelled into the role. He was immediately recalled, and entered the officer corps to begin studying for his new role. He took charge of the Syrian occupation of Lebanon in 1998, and began to be groomed for leadership.

Many have said that he was a reluctant leader, but from the start of his rule in 2000, when his father died, he set about putting his own stamp on the nation. He released many prisoners, began privatizing banks, allowed an independent newspaper to open, and brought the Internet to the country. He stopped the grand military parades of his father's era, and preferred driving himself around the city in his Audi. Along with his glamorous wife Asma, he cultivated the appearance of a people's president, and briefly oversaw what was called "The Damascus Spring."

But it was all a facade, and in only a year his true colors began to show. In 2001, there was a call from academics and students to liberalize even more. They wanted greater freedoms and a new parliament—things Assad was not willing to give. He cracked down, and for the next ten years he picked up his fathers mantle—albeit while still projecting a face of soft spoken innocence to the outside world.

As the Arab Spring began around the region, he intensified the police state, and began using the Shabiha, his infamous death squads. The Shabiha had long been a regular sight in the coastal areas of Latakia and around Damascus, where for decades they had acted as henchmen to the regime. They were the regime's most violent thugs, had long controlled smuggling rings, grown rich under Assad, and were considered untouchables. Their name translates as Black devils, and is also a reference to the unmistakable cars they drove—Blacked out Mercedes, which roared around the country, terrorizing people.

It was the Shabiha who escalated the brutality early in the revolution, and who are blamed for most of the early acts of depravity. More people began disappearing, more innocents were tortured, and more girls were raped, and these obscene acts became another tool in the attempt to placate the people. It was this violence, combined with social media, that slowly brought the world's Sunni fighters to Syria, and the trickle became a stream, which became a river. Clerics throughout the Sunni world encouraged people to help their Syrian brothers, and fueled by Saudi and Gulf money, the war of religions began.

From very early on, Assad latched on to the idea of foreign fighters, as evidence that the opposition were terrorists, and as before he attempted to portray himself as the victim. He claimed to be saving the region from the grasp of radicalization, and while there was some truth to that then, and a lot of truth to it now, it was his own acts that led to this escalation.

The opportunities for intervention certainly presented themselves. When Assad crossed the red line by using debilitating chemical weapons against his own people, nothing was done to help them. If there had been one clear opportunity to remove Assad and prevent his indiscriminate attacks from the air, this was it—but instead a deal was brokered with the help of Assad's allies—the Russians, and Assad agreed to give up his chemicals.

It is absolutely essential for the defeat of ISIS that Assad be removed. He is the galvanizing influence in the country, the reason that people flock to fight. It should be a priority of the United States in the war that goes forward. As Senator John McCain said, "Mr. Assad all but created Islamic State through his slaughter of nearly 200,000 Syrians, and he has knowingly allowed the group to grow and operate with impunity inside the country when it suits his purposes. Until we confront this reality, we can continue to degrade Islamic State in Syria, but Mr. Assad's barbarism will continue to empower it."

Aleppo

© Photo courtesy of Rick Findler

A regular sight in the devastated City of Aleppo, Syria— October, 2012.

By September 2013, the streets of Aleppo were death traps. Gun battles could be heard all along the front lines, and shells and bombs rained down constantly.

On some days, we counted bombs dropping at a rate of ten a minute, and they fell right across the city, spitting shrapnel and engulfing us in smoke. Many people had left the city by then, and the front lines were a ghost town ready for urban warfare.

Whole blocks of buildings had their facades blown off, apartments left open to the street; other buildings, intact but empty, with their curtains billowing out of the windows. Broken water pipes turned roads into debris-clogged rivers. The city was divided into two at that point, and the front lines swayed back and forth, though never by very much. Fighters from both sides, mainly just FSA and regime at that point, were never more than one street away.

One katiba (loosely translated as a battalion) we stayed with had begun talking to their enemies across a courtyard—this often happened, and they would pass the time debating. I remember one fighter telling me in sadness how they would have been friends just a year earlier. Now they were desperately trying to kill each other in what was becoming an increasingly dirty urban war.

Snipers were a constant threat. The city's tall buildings and abandoned homes served as perfect nests, and crossing every small street required a mad dash. We agreed that at every intersection we would count to three then run together, but our fixer, Zaher, once the Syrian national athletic champion, would always begin running at two. Of course this warned the sniper that others were following, and on a few occasions the ping a of bullet would shoot past as we ran. Zaher would stand sheepishly at the other side, pretending he'd misunderstood or miscounted, until we all just started running on one.

Trying to recover dead bodies that had been hit by a sniper's bullet often led to more deaths as snipers would pick off rescuers while they tried to retrieve bodies for burial. Sometimes the bodies would lay out for days, just rotting in the middle of open spaces, unable to be retrieved.

On one of our trips, I remember walking around a corner to find the decapitated body of a man, his windpipe hanging out the top of his neck, lying on a pavement. Sitting alongside his body, clutching a gun, was a thirteen-year-old boy quietly weeping. Nobody knew where he'd come from or what his name was, and the boy was of no relation—he had just sat and cried. Scenes like this were everywhere…

Every few streets were controlled by a different "katiba" and it was hard to always know if they were friendly. We often drove past Jabhat al-Nusra headquarters with cameras hidden and our eyes straight ahead, knowing full well what might happen if we were caught. At every checkpoint we came to we'd hold our breaths, but other than the one occasion when we ended up out of the car on our knees at gunpoint, an error at an FSA checkpoint, we got through.

The last time we were in Aleppo, it was even harder to pinpoint the origin of the fighters. The flags they held, the accents they had, the weapons they carried all pointed to outside influence. I can remember well standing at a food stall away from the front lines one day when up walked a group of foreign fighters. Their clothes, beards, accents stood them out as Yemeni, and we lowered our heads. They received what they wanted and stormed off, having not seen the two foreigners in the corner. That was the last time we went to Aleppo, a city that is demolished, and what little hope there was early on has now faded.

Early Days

There was one opportunity for the United States to intervene, and I believe it was a mistake they did not. Obama had long said that the use of chemical weapons would constitute the crossing of a red line, yet at 2:45 a.m. on the 21st of August, Assad did just that, in a direct challenge to Obama.

The videos which emerged from that attack show in the most graphic detail large numbers of men, women, and children, choking, vomiting, collapsing, and scratching violently. Children screaming because they couldn't explain the pain and the choking, and medics shaking them, unable to do anything, before keeling over themselves. Bodies literally covered the streets, as people slowly dropped and died. Small children and babies were covered by their dead mothers. The bodies were lined up side-by-side in local halls and mosques, and out on the streets, swaddled in rags.

Sarin is an odorless gas, and was dispersed while the people of the eastern Gouda district of Damascus slept. UN chemical weapons inspectors have confirmed that it was used, and UN secretary General Ban Ki-Moon has called it a war crime. He said it was the "most significant confirmed use of chemical weapons against civilians since Saddam Hussein."

It wasn't just the use of gas that should have evoked a

response—ultimately a death is a death and there were many others going on around the country. Instead it was the ultimatum that was laughed at, the red line that was crossed without any response, which defined this. That nothing was done took the teeth out of Obama and he lost his legitimacy. That was when we began to see a turn in the war, it was the tipping point at which the people of Syria gave up on outside help, and turned to extremists.

I believe that the right response would have been a symbolic strike on Assad's air bases and command and control centers. Not to shake him from power immediately, but to reduce his capacity to indiscriminately bomb his people from the air, for that was how he continued to slaughter them. That would have given the still moderate rebel groups (there were some left) precious time to regroup and create a stronger opposition without the need to turn to outsiders. That chance is now gone.

A few tomahawk missiles from the warships in the Mediterranean could have done this with little loss of life. Instead, the whole world, including Putin watched as Obama showed he didn't stand by his word—and Russia particularly learned that now was the time to push the West. I wouldn't be surprised if this gave added incentive for Putin to launch his annexation of the Crimea. It was a shambolic, weak moment in the presidency.

It was right around this time that ISI morphed into ISIS and grew strong. Baghdadi watched from Iraq as other groups hijacked the conflict, and it wasn't long until he too wanted a piece. Initially, his aim had only been to retake western Iraq, but in Syria, he saw the opportunity for much more.

In hindsight, we might say that had the United States focused on the removal of Assad early on, and helped prevent the human tragedy, ISIS may not have had a base to grow in. Or perhaps, had nationalist moderate rebels been trained and armed earlier, we might have prevented the rapid growth of Gulf-funded radicals. The truth is, we don't know if either of these would have done anything, but the West's inaction couldn't have left us in a worse place.

The increasing sectarian nature of the war, these horrible acts committed by Bashar al-Assad and his army, and the vast funds being sent from Saudi Arabia and Gulf states, galvanized thousands of Sunnis to join the extremists, while the videos of babies cut open, prisoners sodomized and other horrific acts proved that Assad was attacking with impunity. Baghdadi was ready to strike.

Jabhat al-Nusra and ISIS

© Photo courtesy of Rick Findler

Syrian rebels in their cave, high in the hills of Idlib province, Syria—April 2012.

Today the other major rebel power in Syria is Jabhat al-Nusra. They are still an official Al-Qaeda franchise in Syria and along with ISIS are the other effective fighting force. While ISIS is now technically fighting against Jabhat al-Nusra, they were once the same group. And the story of ISIS in Syria begins with the creation of Jabhat al-Nusra. The way they split perfectly highlights the complex web of allegiances and power struggles within the war.

In August 2011, Baghdadi, watching the Syrian conflict grow, sent one of his top fighters, Abu Mohammed al-Julani, from Iraq to Syria to establish a presence there. At this point he had only recently taken the reigns at ISI, had not freed the prisoners or established an army, and was still answerable to Zawahiri, the head of Al-Qaeda in Afghanistan.

He had initially stayed out of the Syrian conflict, preferring to establish his caliphate in western Iraq, but as the right conditions arose in Syria, he decided to enter the fray, and arranged for Julani to travel to the northwestern province of Idlib. Julani traveled with eight other fighters in order to establish Jabhat al-Nusra (or Jabhat an-Nuṣrah li-Ahli ash-Shām, meaning "The Support Front for the People of Al-Sham").

Having traveled from Anbar province through Kurdish-controlled territories in the north, Julani and his men set about bringing together many of the jihadi groups that had started to form early on in the conflict. Often these were small groups in scattered towns, but under the umbrella of Jabhat al-Nusra and Al-Qaeda, they quickly began to grow.

Many of these groups had been formed by prisoners released from Sednaya prison at the beginning of the war, and indeed many of them had spent much time on the same floor of this prison. As with Camp Bucca in Iraq, Sednaya prison served as a recruiting and planning location for jihadists, who might otherwise have never met. That Assad would release so many jihadists in a so-called "amnesty" is widely accepted to show his hand in creating the threat of ISIS and Jabhat al-Nusra. Effectively, he needed an enemy at his gates to detract from his own atrocities, and released them knowing they would form jihadi groups.

Among the prisoners released were various fighters who have gone on to become leading players in all the jihadi groups, including leaders within Jabhat al-Nusra and ISIS. According to inmates who were alongside them in the prison, these men were known as leaders even back then, and after being released, their images were aired on Syrian state television, and they were accused of being terrorists and planting bombs. The close historical relationship between Syrian intelligence and extremists suggests they may well have been used again to save Assad.

Jabhat al-Nusra quickly became the most successful fighting force in the country, thanks in large part to the support of Gulf and Saudi money. At this point, support for Jabhat al-Nusra was widely encouraged in all these countries, via social media and television. Thanks to this support, Jabhat al-Nusra began winning decisive battles against Assad in the northeast and especially in Aleppo, and they were soon the dominant jihadist group in the country.

They gained a greater following than the Free Syrian Army, in part because they fed civilians, and gave them oil for cooking and heat as the bitterly cold winter moved in. The FSA always claimed to do this, but never did. Instead, money disappeared into the pockets of leaders or was spent on weapons rather than aid, and so a backlash led to their demise. When we were in Aleppo, all the civilians were talking about the lifeline that Jabhat al-Nusra had given them. They admitted back then that they were radical and enjoyed killing, but praised them as the group that would defeat Assad.

Unlike the soon to be founded ISIS, Jabhat al-Nusra never set out to create a caliphate or impose sharia laws. Instead, it acted as an umbrella organization, often allying with other groups, including moderate FSA battalions for specific attacks and sieges. They were the vanguard of many attacks, launching insurgent style tactics. In their eyes, they were trying to normalize things in the country by defeating Assad—ISIS had other agendas.

In 2013, as Jabhat al-Nusra grew stronger, Baghdadi decided he wanted control, and announced publicly that Julani, who had been leading the group, was his underling. His ambition growing stronger by the day, Baghdadi announced that he was combining the two groups under the name ISIS and taking control. Unwilling to relinquish power, Julani refused, informing him that he would remain leader of Jabhat al-Nusra.

The two began a struggle for power and Julani appealed to Al-Qaeda's Zawahiri to mediate, but despite attempted negotiations between the two, neither side could be convinced to share power. When neither side could accept the division (Zawahiri had sided with Julani) there was an official split—half the forces defected to Baghdadi, while the other half stayed with Julani, and for the first time, ISIS became an independent entity in Syria.

ISIS began kidnapping and killing high Jabhat al-Nusra members, and the infighting escalated, leading to a massive car bomb outside the headquarters of Jabhat al-Nusra in Raqqa. Following this they ceded control of the city to ISIS. ISIS promised them safe passage out, but reneged on the deal and killed 120 outside the city and many more inside, who may have been sympathizers.

To this day, the two groups continue their power struggle for dominance, fighting for control of the strategically important oil fields, for border crossings, and for influence.

Due to ISIS's dominance, many of Jabhat al-Nusra's leaders tacitly support them, and in fact, toward the end of 2014, a few began working together. Of the three main Jabhat al-Nusra leaders, Julani remains the principal one and is said to live in Idlib, and his relationship with ISIS has improved a lot. Abu Malik, the leader of Jabhat al-Nusra in Qalamoun and Damascus, also has good relations with ISIS and remains one of the only leaders actually taking on Assad. Abu Mariya Al-Qahtani is the leader in Dier ez-Zor, but he fought a brutal battle against ISIS for the city, and is very much opposed to ISIS, and now supports the FSA instead—a more nationalist group.

So you can see the vast complexities within the different groups. They fight each other, yet they fight together depending on the battle and the enemy. While they remain separate, a number of people continue defecting from Jabhat al-Nusra to ISIS, and it is often said that the fighters under Abu Malik are just sleeper cells for ISIS.

This is why it's so hard to pinpoint the number of fighters in any group. They are fluid and shift allegiances based on money and power, but ultimately we must see both as grave threats with similar agendas.

After two years of increasingly brutal conflict, Syrians began defecting from other groups to ISIS, who were the most successful. In their eyes, the brutality of life under ISIS, and the harsh sharia rule they imposed, was far better than the threat of Assad. Assad's aerial bombs indiscriminately blanket civilian areas, targeting everyone, but with ISIS the local Sunni population know where they stand. They may have no freedom, but if they adhere to the stringent rules, they will by and large be left alone.

And so aligning with ISIS meant a chance to overthrow the regime, and for many that was enough. Amid the chaos, Syrian fighters see it as the fastest way to victory, but while the people of Syria make decisions based only on this short-term goal, the hierarchy of ISIS is making plans for centuries to come, and defeating Assad is not ISIS's top priority. For them, the establishment of a caliphate stretching from Lebanon to Iraq is the primary goal—as their next move would show.

Kurdish Peshmerga forces walk past a road sign to Mosul shortly after ISIS swept across northern Iraq—June 2014.

CHAPTER FOUR

Iraq Implodes

General Abdullah

In 2013, I met General Abdullah Moses Kardom in Baghdad. The general, complete with thick mustache, portly belly and golden epaulets was a relic from the past, and embodied everything that was wrong with the Iraqi army. His office, filled with chandeliers, gilded grandfather clocks, thick gold-edged rugs, countless flags, embroidered curtains, and vases of fake flowers, was in stark contrast to the bleak barracks outside, where the men had nothing.

As we walked in, General Abdullah strolled around his desk to the center of his vast office. He was watching a sales pitch of military equipment. He had called us in half an hour before our meeting was due to start, and pointed to the corner of the room where we were made to stand quietly. He then paraded around, interrupting the salesman regularly by raising his finger in silence, before checking to see if we had noticed. He would then return to the bank of phones on his sprawling mahogany desk and call somebody in, only to send them away with a wave of his hand without saying a word, before looking over again to check if we had noticed.

The general oversaw the purchase of millions of dollars of a "revolutionary bomb detection device," which turned out to be nothing more than novelty golf ball finders, and which resulted in one of the worst corruption scandals of the time. They had been sold by James McCormick, a retired British policeman who had made seventy-five million dollars selling the devices for forty thousand dollars each, when they cost only twenty dollars to make.

McCormick had just ordered them online before putting them in a fancy box and shipping them to Iraq where they were used on the front line against bomb attacks—General Abdullah had been responsible for their distribution. Amazingly, despite knowing they're useless, every checkpoint in Baghdad continues to use them. "The terrorists don't know they are fake," we were told, "so they are still afraid of them." The terrorists must be the only ones!

How the general kept his job while all of the officers under him lost theirs, is a mystery, and while there's no evidence to suggest he was involved in the scam at all, corruption in Iraq is well documented. What happened next in Iraq, is a direct consequence of the state of the Iraqi army and the endemic corruption that exists from top to bottom.

Iraq Army Flees

"I think what we all probably missed was the degree to which the Iraqi armed forces had eroded and wouldn't stand and face ISIS. I think we all missed that."
—General Dempsey

In June 2014, ISIS grabbed the headlines again, sweeping from Syria through to Iraq, capturing vast areas across the country. As city after city fell, members of Congress called out for support, insisting that if ISIS wasn't hit then, Mosul would fall—sure enough, after having simply looked away, the United States had to watch as ISIS conquered Iraq's second biggest city, Mosul, freed 1440 battle hardened jihadis from prisons, and seized countless battalions worth of United States built heavy weaponry. Tanks, armored vehicles, and artillery filled their storerooms, turning ISIS into a fully equipped modern fighting force overnight, and changing them from terrorist organization to global threat. Along the way, they massacred thousands of soldiers and civilians, leaving their bodies piled up high to rot in the summer sun.

What allowed them to conquer Mosul and so much territory in northern Iraq so quickly was ultimately the state of the Iraqi army—so riddled with corruption and nepotism it simply crumbled. But despite this knowledge, nobody anticipated how great the failure would be—it was monumental!

The Iraqi army had been touted as a great success, and was the very reason the United States was able to pull out of Iraq with its head held high. United States military trainers had voiced concerns but were silenced, and everybody underestimated how tactically advanced ISIS was. This was thanks in large part to the remnants of Saddam's military, and the support of Sunni tribes.

It is no exaggeration to say that Iraqi troops literally dropped their weapons and ran in the face of the ISIS onslaught. The day after the offensive started, I toured some of the bases left empty by Iraqi troops and found the beds unmade, army uniforms and IDs strewn over the floor, and personal belongings left in lockers. Doors were wide open, and taps were still running. Thirty thousand Iraqi soldiers had fled their posts at night, discarding anything that could identify them and leaving large areas free for ISIS to simply walk through. Were it not for Kurdish troops, who mobilized quickly to their fringe towns in the north, taking over abandoned bases, ISIS would have swept a lot farther through the country.

A few days after the blitzkrieg I spoke to one of the soldiers who had fled. Ahmed, who was by then hiding in the northern city of Sulemaniyah, explained life in the army, the days leading up to the ISIS attack, and why they had all fled.

He described how the Iraqi army was so riddled with corruption that they didn't even have to show up at the barracks. That in exchange for half of their four hundred dollar salary, the commander would simply let you stay home. He said that his officers had been crooks who had progressed through nepotism alone, that many didn't have a basic understanding of military tactics, and that many were never present. This is something we see again and again in post invasion Iraq—a country and military built around internal alliances rather than a meritocracy.

Officers buy their ranks, extort money from civilians, and inflate their payrolls and the number of soldiers in their ranks. They sell food and ammo earmarked for their men, which very quickly can end up in the hands of ISIS. It is a sorry state of affairs, and one of the reasons pumping more money into the Iraqi army must only happen on the condition of more oversight. As of November 2014, 1.3 billion dollars had been requested by the Pentagon for the Iraqi army this on top of the twenty-five billion dollars of training and equipment the United States has already given over the last decade.

When ISIS began their push through Iraq, and were approaching Mosul, Ahmed and other soldiers sought guidance from their officers. To their horror, they found the officers in civilian clothing, fleeing, leaving orders for the soldiers to hold the base. "They ran away," Ahmed told me. "So why should I stay and fight for them? Why should I fight for an army that deserts me, that stands for nothing but corruption, and family and money and not Iraq? Why should I die for that army?"

Ahead of ISIS came stories of their brutality toward soldiers and Shiites—decapitation, slaughter, and torture—all true, but carefully managed by ISIS propagandists to spread fear and terror. It worked, and with these tales ringing in their ears, and with countless videos of mass executions and death shared among them, there was no way they were staying to fight. The night after the officers left, the men followed suit.

It had been a military master class. Nobody had seen the attack coming, people had been powerless to stop it, the fast sweeping tactics through the desert had worked, and for the first time people around the world awoke to the real threat that faced them. ISIS had arrived.

Massacre at Badoush

© Photo courtesy of Rick Findler

Helmets of Iraqi soldiers are left discarded following the collapse of their army in June 2014.

As ISIS overran Mosul on June 10, 2014, they had two main targets, the bank and Badoush prison. The bank contained over four hundred million dollars in cash, while Badoush had 1440 battle hardened jihadi prisoners who they needed to bolster their numbers. Unlike the daring raid on Abu Ghraib a year earlier, this time they met no resistance.

The prison had originally been guarded by up to one thousand soldiers and security personnel, including a regiment of the Iraqi army's third division, a regiment of the police, a company of transport vehicles, and a protection force. But after receiving calls from their families begging them to flee, and having watched their superiors leave earlier in the day, the guards all did the same. A few hundred of them had received phone calls directly from ISIS days earlier, threatening their families, and so by the time ISIS forces arrived, nobody remained.

Sitting twenty kilometers to the west of Mosul between the banks of the Tigris river and the A1 highway, Badoush was a massive Saddam-era compound housing twenty-seven hundred prisoners — by the following day, many of them would be dead. Human Rights Watch spoke to some of the twenty men who survived, who recalled their ordeal.

The massacre at Badoush is one of the worst single atrocities in recent years, and shows how little regard ISIS has for human life. It was the first mass execution of Shia prisoners, and one which ISIS hailed as a victory for Allah against the Shia "infidels," but the scenes described by the few survivors paint a torrid and sickening picture.

Having heard that ISIS had taken Mosul, the prisoners began begging to be let out. For hours they banged on the doors of their cells, screaming and shaking the bars, but there was nobody left in the prison. The Shia prisoners knew what would happen if they were caught, and they tore their fingers trying to bring down their cells. Finally, as dawn broke, some managed to break their locks, and released many of the others. They sprinted out of the gates, and down the road—but too late. They came face-to-face with hundreds of ISIS fighters tearing down the road towards them, black flags flying from every car.

The prisoners were quickly rounded up, and those

who attempted to run away were shot. Herded into buses, they were driven into the desert before being split into Sunni and Shia. Many of the Shia prisoners tried to join the Sunnis, but were unable to recite specific prayers, and were caught. They were marched out to the desert in a line so long, say some, that they couldn't see the front of the column—their heads were bowed, and their hands tied. They approached a ravine and were lined up, side by side—around one thousand men in total, and told to count themselves out. Some of the survivors heard as far as the three hundreds, some the six hundreds, but the counting went on, finally going quiet at 960. Standing there in silence, they began to recite the Koran, praying for a swift death—they knew what was coming. One overheard a fighter asking the leader "El-Hajji" (an honorific title given to someone who has done the pilgrimage to Mecca) what to do.

"Kill them two by two," he said, as they heard men approaching behind. "No, do it ten by ten," he called out, as the men took their places. Finally he shouted "Just kill them all." And the bullets began to pour. There were about two ISIS fighters for every five prisoners, and as their guns erupted, the noise was shattering. The bodies dropped down the hill, and many prisoners tried to throw themselves down before being shot. For fifteen minutes the firing continued into the ravine unabated, left and right, up and down. One survivor remembers the blood and brains of the next man all over him.

Some tried to hide under corpses as the pile mounted, some tried to run; all were shot down. When they had finished shooting, the fighters came down and continued firing. They lit sticks, and went down the line, setting clothing and bodies alight. Many weren't quite dead and tried to hold back their pain, lying motionless, many couldn't, and were shot. Finally, when the ISIS fighters ran out of bullets, they left, and the scene went quiet. After an hour or so, the few who had survived limped off into the desert; they wouldn't go back to the road. Most had been shot somewhere, and as they walked they slowly dropped dead one-by-one. It is believed that around twenty survived, leaving behind 940 slaughtered bodies. It was to be the first of many such mass executions.

Today Badoush is again a prison, but now it's used to hold and rape women. Hundreds of Yazidi girls who were captured around Mount Sinjar were sent there before being sold like cattle to foreign fighters; from there many are sent across into Syria. Some reports suggest that beauticians are brought from Mosul to make the girls look prettier for the fighters, dressing them up and putting makeup on them and instructing them to be subservient for the fighters.

Declaration of Caliphate

© Photo by Sipa Press/REX

Abu Bakr al-Baghdadi, preaching at a mosque on the day he announced himself as Caliph. Mosul, Syria.

"This group, ISIS, is not Islamic first of all, and the caliphate they have declared is a fraudulent one."
—John Brennan, Director of CIA

A couple of weeks after ISIS took over Mosul, on June 29, 2014, Baghdadi appeared in a Mosul mosque and declared the creation of the caliphate, with himself as Caliph. The move took everyone by surprise, but the timing of the declaration was very clever. ISIS had recently captured a third of Iraq, they were on the offensive in Syria, and they had begun to tear down the border posts along the Syrian-Iraqi border; effectively they were doing well, and this was the time to take advantage of it—to stamp authority over the wider jihadi movement.

However, the move was frowned upon by the global ideologues who saw Baghdadi as little more than a power hungry upstart, and ISIS received very little support from any prominent jihadists. Most other groups believe that he is not descended from the Quraish tribe, the leading Arab tribe from whom all Caliph's must descend and who are directly related to the prophet Muhammad. At the time only a group in Indonesia and one element within Al-Qaeda in the Islamic Megrab (AQIM) offered allegiance, along with a few independent clerics—including the British preacher Anjem Choudary.

By announcing the new caliphate just fourteen months after Baghdadi created and claimed leadership over ISIS, he was effectively setting himself up as a ruler "by the order of God." He was stating that he had become "commander of all the faithful" and successor to the prophet Muhammad. A spokesman for ISIS, Abu Mohammed al-Adnani, declared that this was the "jihadi's long running dream," and it was the first time in ninety years that an "Islamic State" had been established.

He also claimed that all requirements to proclaim a caliphate and claim leadership over all Muslims had been met. Among them it is said the leader must have complete rule over a territory, have funds, an army, and a population under his control. That most of his population was subjugated was irrelevant.

The reasons for establishing a caliphate are varied. Firstly, in doing so Baghdadi claimed that every Muslim must pledge allegiance to him; that he was God's chosen one, and that any groups that didn't were to be attacked. This is important, because as the conflict had grown, fewer and fewer battles were actually fought between ISIS and Assad, effectively leaving Baghdadi to take over other groups and consolidate power.

The battle had become not a war against an oppressive regime or even the sectarian one he claimed it was, but rather about the creation of a state. By doing this, he effectively told all other jihadi groups, including Al-Qaeda central, that they lacked legitimacy, and that it was now lawful to kill those who had not sworn allegiance—it is this law that drives his many fighters to kill other Muslims, and which has created the tensions that exist within the global jihadi movement.

But the move was also a nod to its own core group of followers, the younger jihadis. Those who were drawn to this idea of a nation state, of redrawing lines, of revolution; those who wanted to create something new when so much in their own countries—low employment, low salaries—was going badly. These were the disaffected angry youths who had no connection to established ideologues around the world, who they saw droning on about ancient texts and hiding away in mountain caves.

ISIS, as we will see later, always sought to consolidate and expand its appeal among young jihadists; it sought to harness those who felt disconnected from the established movement, which had over the last decade disappeared. In their eyes, ISIS is the group that gets things done. It has the most presence on social media, and it appears attractive and active, and makes them feel important. It is this grassroots movement that ISIS has managed to harness around the world.

As one jihaidi tweeted to an older cleric in London, who had criticized the establishment of a caliphate,

"You're there eating fish and chips in London, don't talk to me about the establishment of a caliphate. We're actually doing it!" This is a widely held feeling among the ISIS core. So the declaration both galvanized some and pushed away others, but Baghdadi had weighed up the options and decided that the benefits outweighed the negatives.

The Koran

CHAPTER FIVE

Twisted Ideology

"Even when killing an innocent, they scream, 'Allahu Akbar.' These Islamists are going back to the seventh century, especially in a radical way and with war... The majority of Muslims are shocked by the actions of these terrorists, but many see them as authentic Muslims, and so few speak clearly against them...The astonishing thing, as you said at the very beginning, is that they are fighting the immorality of the West and Western hedonism. But they are doing many more immoral things in the name of Islam."

—Jesuit Father Samir Khalil Samir,
A leading scholar of Islam

ISIS ideology is rooted in ancient Islam, but it also has a habit of swaying with their desired appearance. There's no doubt that they follow a hard line, Salafi form of Islam, but they also tap into a lot of ancient religious prophecies for the sake of rallying their followers. They use countless religious texts to justify their actions, from the obscure to the archaic.

At their core, they want to go back to an early interpretation of Islam—one best defined by the Wahhabism which is practiced in Saudi Arabia. They reject all forms of non-Muslim government, education, and law (yet desperately need Western-trained engineers, telecom systems, internet providers, and banking systems to survive). They claim they want to purify Islam and in turn the world, and that they are allowed to slaughter apostates or "non-believers" who stand in their way—this includes anyone who has not sworn allegiance to the Caliph, including fellow Muslims.

Yet much of their rhetoric also evokes a pre-apocalyptic sense of war—they see themselves as the final army that will wipe all enemies away by either enslaving them or killing them. They constantly refer to biblical clashes between crusaders and Islamic armies on the battlefields of Syria, and claim to be re-fighting them. Such is the importance of this rhetoric, that they have gone out of their way to capture towns (such as Dabiq) which are not strategically important, but which serve their own propaganda.

Their scriptures, the Koran and the Hadith, are not intended to be guidelines, but literal word. This absoluteness is the definition of fundamentalism. As such, they are able to justify almost any action they deem necessary thanks to a very flexible interpretation of their "holy books."

Ironically, they claim to be righting the wrongs committed by others—the "evil" West, Shia

Muslims, and Gulf monarchies are chief among their enemies—and in doing so they think nothing of slaughtering anyone who gets in their way.

It's important to remember that almost all influential Islamic leaders around the world refuse to acknowledge ISIS as a caliphate and even refuse to accept their legitimacy. Yet it does have a large following among young Muslims the world over. What they have managed to do successfully is bring radical Islam into the twenty-first century and make it appealing to young people. Whereas previously the global jihad movement was based from a cave high in the mountains of Afghanistan, and preachers droned on for hours about religious scripts, ISIS has sidelined much of this. They portray themselves as saviors of Islamic civilization, they have glitzy video games that look like TV shows, and they try to make killing lookcool.

Let's also not forget that the core leadership is made up of Saddam-era ex-Ba'athists, many of whom followed a very nationalistic program under Saddam Hussein. It really seems that many of them have joined ISIS out of a desire to return to power, rather than for a pure religious purpose. That being said, their leaders do shun most human comforts—which might possibly have more to do with the drones overhead than with desire.

Many of their followers are attracted not by their religious zeal, but by their ability to fight Assad. It does seem as if, in the long-term, there may be a backlash against the strict form of Sharia law they seek to impose.

That they will kill hundreds of fellow Sunnis for

opposing them is evidence of their willingness to seek power over unity, and that they will deal with the Allawite Assad regime by selling oil is evidence of their willingness to put those religious differences aside whenever it suits them.

CHAPTER SIX

Military Prowess
The Greatest Weapon is Fear

"If you put two brigades on the ground right now with US forces, they would push ISIS back into Syria in a heartbeat."
—General Anthony Zinni,
Former Cent Com Commander-in-Chief

We were huddled against a wall just fifty meters from Assad's forces under heavy fire, unable to move. Three of us were trying to squeeze behind one reinforced pillar, while the rest of the cinder block wall crumbled under incoming fire. The wall running away from us on our left was being targeted by heavy caliber machine gun fire from our right, and would explode sporadically as another bullet hit home. We were well and truly penned in, and I remember looking over at Rick and the line of rebels crouched alongside us, and thinking we'd really messed things up.

It was November 2012, and it was freezing. We had arrived in Syria from Turkey just a couple of hours earlier and had heard of an imminent attack by the rebels on Minnagh Airport, just south of the town of Azaz. We rushed there as fast as we could.

Minnagh Airbase was a hugely symbolic target for the rebels. From the base, Assad launched his deadly, indiscriminate air attacks on local civilians, and the rebels needed to capture it if there was to be any respite. But Assad, who knew how important his airbases were for his campaign, continued to supply the soldiers inside by air, and continued dropping reinforcements by night. Every night we would watch as fighter jets bombed the fields surrounding the base, giving cover to helicopters coming into land, the flashes lighting up the night sky and shaking the walls some miles away.

That first day we arrived, the head of the FSA battalion in the region granted us permission to move forward to the frontline and watch the imminent attack, so we had driven through the abandoned villages to the north of the base, sped dangerously down a muddy road covered by an Assad tank, and finally moved forward on foot through the remnants of the shelled out buildings. It was an eerie place; we knew what force lay ahead, but could see nobody around. We crept closer to the wall of the airbase, and making it to the front, peeked through a hole to see what lay ahead.

It had been a ghost town when we'd arrived— silent— when suddenly bullets started to fly from all directions. Assad's forces had changed position, flanking the front wall and, we were suddenly trapped. They had our escape route covered from their watch towers and the only way back was across the open field the way we'd come—but this was under fire. We knew it wouldn't be long till an RPG exploded on our position, and so after some quick radio calls, we made the decision to run for it.

The author runs from incoming fire during the siege of Minnagh, northern Syria—January 2013

One by one we raced across the field, heads low, bullets flying, until scrambling over a pile of rocks at the other side. Reaching it, we threw ourselves over and turned to watch the last man crossing behind us, only to see something I will never forget: the commander skipping along through the bullets, laughing as he came.

That said, its all about the mind frame of the fighters—slightly twisted by battle, and with an acceptance of death. This time he was lucky though. We moved up to the roof of an adjoining abandoned building and watched for a while as snipers try to pick off Assad soldiers—it was as if nothing had happened.

That day in Minnagh, I was reminded that nothing happens on time in the Middle East. It took ten months for the rebels to finally capture that base, but it only fell when the FSA were joined by the ISIS leader Abu Omar Shishani and his brutal gang of Chechens. When we had been there, it had been under the sole control of badly funded, badly armed rebels with little knowledge of tactical warfare—but when Shishani arrived, he took control of the operation, and the base fell soon after.

He rigged trucks with high explosives, coated them in metal plating, and from the day he arrived systematically obliterated Minnagh defenses by sacrificing as many men as it took. It says everything about the military zeal of ISIS and its battle hardened, experienced core, versus the ability of other rebel groups.

Shishani is an almost mythical figure in ISIS and Syria now, not least because of his looks—he has a long bright red beard and hair—or for his nationality—and as his name suggests, he hails from Chechnya. He is known as the best fighter in ISIS and is personally responsible for countless victories—and countless deaths. Today he is the ISIS military chief of staff, and northern commander. He may also sit on the Shura council.

I spoke to an ISIS defector who had fought alongside him and he told me about the man they dubbed, "Red Beard."

He was born Tarkhan Tayumurazovich Batirashvili in Georgia in 1986, in a small mountain hut with no electricity or water, and was raised a Christian. He grew up as a shepherd in the Pankisi Gorge—a famous way point for Chechen militants fighting Russia in the nineties. Chechens at the time were (and still are) heavily abused by Russia, which sought to crack down on the

Islamic rebellion. According to his father, from a young age, Shishani began helping ethnic Chechens sneak into Russia to fight, even joining them on some missions.

Pictured on ISIS's website, Abu Omar al-Shishani, the red-bearded Chechen who rose to the top of the ISIS military structure. Chechen fighters are known as the most vicious and effective soldiers.

After school he joined the Georgian army where he quickly excelled at tactics and weaponry. He was promoted to a sergeant in a special intelligence unit, and was on the path to becoming an officer when war against Russia broke out in 2008. He spent the duration at the front lines doing reconnaissance of Russian tanks where he honed his skills, spending days alone at the front observing enemy movements.

After the war that he was diagnosed with tuberculosis. He had to leave the army, and was forbidden from rejoining. This was the beginning of his move toward Islam and jihad. He still hated Russia, and wanted to strike at it in any way he could, so when the Syrian conflict started, he moved there to fight Assad, who he saw as an extension of the Kremlin. It was here that he really began his move to fundamentalism, and as he excelled on the battlefield, and added more and more fighters to his group Jaish al-Muhajireen wal-Ansar. He and other Chechen militants, quickly became known for their brutality—decapitating countless prisoners, and showing an aggression on the battlefield that exceeds even other ISIS members.

Soon after his victory at Minnagh, he joined with Baghdadi, and his goal became not just the defeat of Assad, but the creation of the Caliphate. The shepherd boy from Georgia had come a long way. The last time his father heard from him was in 2014, when he called to say he was married to a Chechen woman and had a daughter named Sophia. When his father told him he was still a practicing Christian, he hung up. He is known to have been based in a villa near Aleppo, but according to two men who fought with him, he also sleeps with his men on the floor, eats with them, and laughs with them. Even those who have left ISIS praised him as a great leader.

It is no exaggeration to say that Shishani and other battle hardened members of ISIS are the ones who brought the early military success. They are the initial core of eight hundred fighters, who, bolstered by two thousand released prisoners, led the charge across Iraq, using their terror and tactics to win quickly. They were the tip of the ISIS spear, vicious, ruthless and lethal, and their early successes were monumental in bringing about their so-called caliphate.

Tactics

Today, ten man groups of new fighters each have one of these Chechen or Libyan fighters leading, guiding them, teaching them. The Libyans are also known as highly skilled fighters from their battles against Qaddafi a few years earlier. Depending on the countries of origin, they often fight with different styles. For example, battles led by Libyans tend to be much tougher warfare—face-to-face fighting, brutal street to street gun battles; while those led by the Chechens usually involve long, drawn out tactical maneuvers, sneaking up to the enemy and fighting over a longer period of time. They all use Google maps, Google earth, and GPS devices to draw up detailed plans of their attacks. They communicate via the Internet and by phone, with a constant surplus of SIM cards. I've seen rebel fighters with bin bags full of them, and they change them almost every few calls.

All ISIS battalions now use suicide bombers as their first form of attack, either to breach a wall, enter a base, destroy a checkpoint, or free prisoners, before then streaming in through the hole, killing everything they see, and wreaking carnage. Those chosen to commit these suicide attacks are honored and eager to do so. I've been told that families of suicide bombers are paid thirty-six hundred dollars, though those without families and the foreign fighters say they would do it for free. Suicide bombing is without doubt one of ISIS's strongest weapons—and it's almost impossible to stop one man in a vest or carrying an RPG from firing at close range when he doesn't mind being killed.

As soon as they've taken a town, they immediately spread countless IEDs throughout the town, making counterattack almost impossible. They cover the towns with snipers, and most importantly make sure the local population stays to be used as human shields. They move their fighters and adapt their methods depending on the size of the enemy or the locations.

Decentralization

They also have other elements working in their favor that make them such a powerful force. They have a decentralized military command, and trust their well experienced commanders to make the right moves when given a target. Meanwhile, the Iraqis and the Kurds are stifled by their lack of a command and control structure, waiting for precise orders from high up before making any moves—As General Abdullah Kardom of the Kurdish forces said to me, "basic structure is one of the things we desperately need United States help for."

This decentralization means it's very hard to judge their next move, and allows ISIS to dictate the terms of engagement. On numerous occasions, they have surprised their enemies with unexpected, and possibly brash moves, such as attacking the Kurds in the north rather than continuing south, continuing to strike Kobane when its strategic importance is questionable, and expanding in numerous directions at once through the west of Iraq and around Baghdad. This changeable tactic has both helped and hindered them, and is central to their policy of "baqiya wa tatamaddad"—"remaining and expanding"—whereby they never stop moving or fighting in their attempt to consolidate and grab land.

It's helped them by preventing enemies from grouping in one place—instead they've had to spread along ISIS lines. It also means they can't be attacked in one location as each team operates on its own, moving and keeping enemies on edge, for example along the thirteen hundred kilometer border that ISIS shares with the Kurds, where it's impossible to know where they will attack next. They move up and down the lines in pickup trucks before regrouping and launching strikes randomly along the border. It has to be said that while this worked very well at first, it also spread them thin in various places—and is now harder to do with United States jets over head.

The knowledge and experience of ex-Saddam officers also gives ISIS major military know-how, but primarily it was the decentralization of their structure combined with the fact that ISIS was stronger than any other armies, which meant the territory was ripe for the picking. During their early victories they never once faced a unified army or any effective fighting force: the Iraqi army was useless and crumbled, the Syrian army never really fought them, the Kurds may have been brave, but simply didn't have the experience or weapons, while Turkey, along with Saudi Arabia and other Gulf states were simply too worried about domestic unrest to risk putting their necks out. Meanwhile other rebel groups, except Jabhat al-Nusra, simply paled in comparison to them, and either joined them or were killed.

The Defector

In a small apartment in Gazientep, Turkey, Abu Almouthanna described the world inside ISIS: the blood lust, the decapitations, the killings, and the camaraderie. He did so without shame, but with great sadness. He told me how he regretted his actions and was telling his story to make amends.

Abu Almouthanna is one of only a handful of defectors to escape from ISIS, a few hundred at the most, who have lived to tell the tale. Often they are hunted down and killed along the border with Turkey, and if not their families are punished in their stead. This is Abu's story:

He was born in 1986 in Raqqa, now the capital of ISIS in Syria. Like his parents, grandparents, and great-grandparents, he had been a farmer. He remembers a happy home—poor and under a dictatorship—but happy. Soon after the revolution began, there was a knock at his door. Soldiers grabbed him, beat his elderly father, arrested him, and took him to Damascus. He hadn't been a leader of the uprising, merely one of the many people caught in its midst—demanding better rights and more freedom.

For ten months he was tortured—he was hung up by his arms for hours every day, and deprived of sleep, and had his nails and toenails pulled out, and his skin flayed. He was forced to share cells with up to twelve others, many of whom were beaten to death. One day, he was simply released and allowed to go home, and he joined the Free Syrian Army (FSA), and was set on his way to war.

"There was such anger in me then, that I wanted to fight," he said. "I wanted to kill." And that's just what he did. He began by attacking regime bases and joining the fledgling insurgency in the hills. He fought with everything he could against the Alawite oppressors—but soon the FSA was unable to keep up, and slowly he noticed other groups arriving, better equipped, better armed, better funded. Jabhat al-Nusra grew strong in his area, and he decided to join.

They immediately started faring better, launching large attacks on army bases. He remembers praying with the suicide bombers before they blew themselves up, before then charging after them on foot to kill the rest. He'd never seen a "martyr" before.

After only four months, ISIS defeated his Jabhat al-Nusra battalion in Raqqa without a bullet fired, and 2000 of them simply changed their name and became ISIS. "I was happy to move to ISIS," he told me. "They had even more money, and the best weapons—other than that they were the same as Jabhat al-Nusra."

He swore allegiance to Baghdadi, meeting his regional emir in the countryside with hundreds of other new fighters. "I put my hands in his and recite the code, 'I swear my allegiance to the prince—al Khalifa al Shaikh Abdullah Ibraheem Ben Awwad Ben Ibraheem Ben Ali Ben Buhammad al Badri—and give him my loyalty and obedience in all matters.'"

He was sent to the countryside for forty days of training led by foreign fighters—Chechens and Afghans—the experienced ones. The training was hard, mainly in weapons, but also physical and tactical. They slept in a farm building as a dormitory, side by side on blankets that covered the floor, waking at 4:30 a.m. for early prayers followed by physical training from 6 a.m. to 8 a.m. There were two training sessions a day, and bedtime was at 10 p.m. For training they were put into ten man groups; usually with mixed nationalities, but Chechens, Uzbeks, Afghans, and Tajiks were often together, so they could understand each other.

They leapt over walls, crawled under logs, and practiced drills, ambushes, maneuvers. They ran at night, and stopped only to pray. The food was plentiful and good—large stews, rice, and meat every day, made by the women and children. He was given clothes and boots and his own gun. "I felt like a real soldier," he told me. He was being paid around $150 a month.

He met scores of other jihadis while training, though none was allowed to use their real name. During this time, he lived with three French fighters and a British man. Their Arabic was basic, but they were given regular lessons to help them improve. He said they were the most radicalized among the group; they had come not with a great knowledge of the Koran, but with the most aggressive motives and blood lust. From day one they joked about cutting heads, bleeding necks, and making the enemy cry.

He fought with ISIS for the next fourteen months, in countless battles, some short—a couple of days—others long, including the battle for Markada, which took five months. Six hundred ISIS fighters were killed and about the same number from the FSA—the same FSA they had once fought with.

For him this was the "unforgettable" battle. By the

end, they were killing everything and everyone they found. Women, children—anyone left in the town. "We walked from house to house, it was easy," he said. "We had been in battle—we were angry, they had killed us, so we killed them." He denied killing any children himself.

Battles were good places to make friends, and afterwards the fighters would talk about the fighting and the enemy—recounting adventurous actions, heroic charges, people they'd killed, or the lucky ones who had been killed. So many fighters volunteered to die as martyrs that he never was asked—"there were too many people who wanted to do it."

If someone was injured he was well treated at a local private hospitals. Foreign fighters came as doctors and nurses and they took over whole hospitals for the fighters—if it was very serious, they would go to Turkey and pretend to be FSA. The hospitals there didn't really check.

They were almost always making jokes—about women, fighting, or killing their enemies. The camaraderie amongst them was "special…." he said. "They were good friends there." And many people got wives. Yazidi girls were sent by truck to Raqqa and married against their will, usually to foreigners. "The emir gives them as a gift. Then they do with them as they want. Tunisians take two or three."

When in the capital of Raqqa, he was treated well, brought drinks and food by shopkeepers and passersby, and he was never asked to pay for anything. He claimed the people of Raqqa were not afraid of him or the other fighters.

He spent some time with his friends hanging out

in the prisons. He said they were always full and that torture went on in every room in front of other prisoners. "Many took pleasure from it." These were not prisoners from battle, rather just people living under ISIS who had broken laws. Mainly they beat them with electric sticks, whip, and rods, but they also cut and burned bodies.

After one battle, they did take prisoners—three hundred of them. They held them for a day in a building outside town, before mowing them all down with guns. "I felt bad" he said, "but we didn't know what to do with them." There were women and children among the prisoners, and they just left them in the building where they'd been killed.

He watched many decapitations, and people would argue about who could cut the head off—sometimes they used it as a test to see who was truly with them, to test new recruits. They often filmed each other decapitating people and then watched the video back later, commenting on the technique. But Abu Almouthanna claims not to have decapitated anyone. "I don't believe in that," he said.

Slowly he began to realize that ISIS wasn't focusing on fighting the regime, they were just taking territory from other groups and killing them, and he was not okay with this. "They were innocent." He had signed up to kill Shia, Kurds, and other fighters, but not FSA or children, and he felt bad about fighting other Syrian rebel groups—of which some of his friends fought for. "It was fighting between tribes, not for religion."

When he made the decision to go, he asked his emir for two days leave to see his family. Because he had been with them for a long time, this was granted. His cousin came to pick him up and drove him to the border, from where he fled to Gazientep. He is looking for work now, "maybe at a restaurant."

He says he's sorry for the innocents he killed, and I believe him, but he would happily to kill again. "Who are your enemies now?" I asked. "Anybody who fights me, anybody who tries to stop us…. Americans, Yazidis, Kurds, Christians. If they have a gun I will kill them."

Militias

© Photo courtesy of Rick Findler

Syrian rebel fighters look out over Minnagh Airbase.

In June of 2014, Ali Saeed heard that ISIS was approaching Baghdad. Inside the city, the rumor mill was high, and Ali had heard from various people that they were just a few miles away. Stories were running wild about the sleeper cells waiting to ignite the city, about the caches of arms they had hidden away, and people were afraid.

Like many others in Baghdad, he was a Shia and knew what would happen if ISIS arrived—they'd be brutally murdered, and their children and wives raped and enslaved. Baghdad was already facing daily bomb attacks from Sunnis, and the gossip was not hard to believe. Soon, he was sure, there would be fighting in the streets. "I was preparing for the worst," he said, "and had already bought guns for the house."

As the Iraqi army fell away in the face of the marauding terrorists, the leading Shia cleric in Iraq, Grand Ayatollah Ali al-Sistani, issued a fatwa, a religious decree, calling for Shias to "defend the country, its people, the honor of its citizens and its sacred places." Thousands heeded his call and took up arms, rallying to recruitment centers—including Ali.

Sistani was once dubbed the most influential figure in the country. It was he who called for the writing of a new constitution after 2003, and then encouraged Iraqis to vote in 2005. Shias followed his every word, and so after he issued his fatwa, every Shia considered it his duty to enlist—Iraqi President Abadi estimated that one million Iraqi Shias flocked to fill the void left by the Iraqi army. These militias would soon become as brutal as ISIS.

A shop keeper by trade, Ali, forty-six years old, hadn't held a gun in decades. He had been a conscript in Saddam's army, of lowly rank, but that was a long time ago. He was duty bound to comply though, so he signed up in the al-Hasd al Sha'bi forces—the popular mobilization forces. After re-training, he was reassigned to a Shia militia about thirty miles south of Baghdad who were fighting against ISIS. It was here that he became "a Shia religious warrior."

As the fighting intensified, the violence worsened, and the Shia militias, operating outside the jurisdiction of the army, began escalating the violence. This had actually been happening for some time inside Baghdad, as people tried to rid their Shia districts of Sunnis— Sunnis started simply disappearing in a growing number.

Before long, Ali and the five hundred odd men in his militia were fighting in an all out sectarian war, taking out their anger on innocent Sunni villagers as well as ISIS. "We know that they all supported ISIS. We knew they wanted to help them take Baghdad, and so we had to stop them." To do this, they began razing villages to the ground, and killing civilians, in a growing tit-for-tat war.

The militias began burning farmland and villages within a twenty mile radius of Baghdad. They call these areas the "Kill zones," and anybody found within them are considered enemies. Eighty thousand Sunnis have now had to leave their homes in the no-man's-land and flee; and its easy to imagine that many of the men with nowhere else to go have now joined ISIS.

There are countless videos online of Shia militias, in their distinctive uniforms, fighting around Iraq. In one, a commander stands over the rotting bodies of men, who do not appear to be fighters, and when asked why he hadn't buried them, answers, "Those terrorists do not deserve to be buried. Let the dogs eat their flesh. They help to kill our men."

These militias are the stalwart supporters of the Iraqi government—but really they answer to Iran. Around the country, they are fighting ISIS, but not under the banner of Iraq, under the banner of the Shia. They don't wear Iraqi uniforms; instead they wear a mix of military fatigues with the insignia of Shia brigades. And they also call themselves jihadists—for them this is a religious war, and it is happening around the country.

From Kurdish areas in the north, to southern and eastern areas in Diyala, Shia militia are not just clearing towns, they're burning them, proudly daubing their names on the walls of towns they clear. This is a problem which will breed more hatred in the long-term, and is another reason why any solution to the ISIS problem is so far away. In many cases, the families left homeless are first pushed out by ISIS, then their homes are destroyed by the militias—it's leaving countless people caught between two evils.

It is another of the war's great ironies that these militias fighting against ISIS in Iraq are the same Shia militias fighting against US-backed rebels in Syria. "Many of the men I have fought with were fighting in Syria before they came back here," Ali acknowledged. They are also in many cases the same Shia fighters who fought against the United States after the invasion of 2003, and now we fight both with and against them.

And this again points to the very significant role played by Iran, who has been the major force behind the creation of these Shia militias. Hoshiyar Zebari, a Kurd who is also deputy Prime Minister of Iraq, has said of Iran, "I think they are paying their salaries. Their food, their clothes and weapons and so on. Over one billion dollars since June for the militias."

Despite the fear and the rumors flowing around Baghdad, and the suggestion that the city might fall, it was never going to. It meant too much to too many people. But the scaremongering was a good way of mobilizing thousands of Shias to take arms. Despite the initial scares as ISIS began their push through Iraq, Baghdad's defenses were always solid—it is effectively ringed in steel—with only a few main corridors in and out. Baghdad is predominantly Shia, and for ISIS to succeed in a city of that size, they'd need more support among the population—support they wouldn't get.

Secondly, the United States knows that to lose Baghdad means losing the country, and despite their dillydallying early on, at this they drew the line. They were willing to respond swiftly and decisively when the Baghdad Airport was approached, flying apache gunships from the airport, where hundreds of United States troops were based, whenever ISIS approached.

Hezbollah

Iran's main military proxy in the region is the Lebanese based Hezbollah, and while talking about militias it's worth saying a few words about their role in Syria. Ultimately, when early on in the Syrian conflict, Assad's forces were being pressurized by rebel groups—in some cases United States-backed rebel groups—it was Iranian and Hezbollah's support which allowed them to hold on.

The United States responded to Hezbollah's involvement (which it classifies as a terrorist organization) by placing more sanctions on the group. As early as

August 2012, a Treasury Department statement said, "This action highlights Hezbollah's activities within Syria and its integral role in the continued violence the Assad regime is inflicting on the Syrian population."

We have to consider that, if Iran had not stepped in to shore up the brutal regime of Assad so early on, the moderate rebels may have been more successful, the regime might have fallen, and ISIS may have had less of a breeding ground in which to operate. It's a big if, but their involvement also galvanized thousands of Sunnis from around the world to flock to what they saw as an increasingly sectarian battle.

Today it's estimated that anywhere from seven thousand to twenty thousand Hezbollah fighters are fighting in Syria, and there's no doubt that without their support, the Assad regime would be severely hampered. I believe that for there to be any kind of solution here, and if the West is to stand a chance of countering ISIS, Assad first needs to go. For that to happen Iran needs to stop supporting his regime, both financially, and also via its proxy Hezbollah.

Afghans

Iran has also been accused of sending Afghan prisoners held in jail in Iran to fight in Syria. A few were caught by FSA fighters and pulled out of the rubble of a home following defeat, and interviewed about why they were there. They told the interviewers that they had been in Iran illegally and arrested for various crimes such as drug dealing and theft. The Iranian government gave them two options: be deported to Afghanistan, where as Shia they risked being killed, or to fight in Syria for six hundred dollars a month—a huge amount for them. And so in a strange twist, early on in the conflict there were 450 Afghan fighters on the side of the Assad regime fighting in Syria, under the direct leadership of an Iranian commander—who according to them was not only in charge of leading them, but also shooting them if they tried to escape. Nothing shows quite like this the twisted involvement of nations in this cauldron of war.

CHAPTER SEVEN

Kidnapped and Murdered

One image in particular defines the brutality of ISIS, and it is seared into our collective minds. It's an image that embodies their cruelty and violence, and that in large part galvanized the West into action. It's that of Jim Foley, kneeling in the sand before his murderer, dressed in an orange jumpsuit but still tall, proud, and defiant. Similar images and videos followed, and each was a deliberate attempt to provoke. Jim Foley, David Haines, David Henning, Peter Kassig, and Steven J. Sotloff.

I don't want to describe those videos here; I don't think I have to, nor do I believe that they should be viewed—but they did play an important role in everything that's happened since, and this, and for so many other reasons, the lives of these men are important. I want to write about each man as the book goes on, in their own words, and in the words of the people around them.

Few people can ever know what it's like to be held by ISIS, and nobody can share the fear they must have felt or begin to know what they went through. However, some prisoners held alongside them were eventually released (their ransoms paid by governments), or swapped for other prisoners, and these people have shed some light on what happened inside. In total twenty-three Western hostages have been kidnapped, including aid workers, and all of the European prisoners (other than the English) have been freed—Germans, Italians, French, Spanish, Danish, and Swiss. One unnamed female American aid worker aged twenty-six, remains in captivity. And the policy of paying ransoms remains controversial.

Jim Foley

© Photo by Jonathan Pedneault/EYEPRESS/REX

Jim Foley, journalist, murdered by ISIS in Syria, August 19, 2014.

Jim, forty-years-old, was the eldest of five children from Rochester, New Hampshire. Initially a teacher, he became drawn toward conflict zones and to telling the stories of those caught up in them. In 2011, he was abducted in Libya while covering the fall of Qaddafi's regime, and spent several weeks in a prison in Tripoli before being released. It wasn't long afterward that he returned to front line reporting, and on November 22, 2012, he was captured.

His good friend Peter Bouckaert, Emergency Director at Human Rights Watch, remembers him like this:

"Jim wasn't the kind of journalist who flew in, filed a few stories, and flew out. When Jim went in, he wanted to live with the local people, share their suffering, and tell their stories. He would commit months to different places, traveling around with local taxis and making local friends. As a former teacher, Jim knew how to connect with people: he could de-escalate the wildest of situations and always seemed able to win the trust of those who mattered.

"I wish there was no video showing his brutal execution to haunt his family and friends forever. It is unbearable to think of Jim's final terror-filled moments, designed by the Islamic State to horrify us all. It is unbearable to think that there are still other hostages in the hands of the Islamic State, hostages kept for the same purpose. It is unbearable to think of the hundreds of mostly nameless Iraqis and Syrians who have suffered the same fate as Jim at the hands of the Islamic State, but Jim would want us to think of them.

"Goodbye, dear Jim, and we will remember you for the beauty of your life well lived and not its brutal end."

Jim and John Cantlie were kidnapped together near the Syrian town of Binish in the northwestern province of Idlib, on November 22, 2012. They'd had a successful trip in-country and were heading back to Turkey when they were grabbed. They had been filing their work at an Internet cafe in the town, when they left for the border, flagging a passing taxi outside. Shortly after they left the village, on a country road amid the barren, rocky landscape, a van sped up behind them and armed men jumped out. They refused to open the door, but finally, as the men began firing their weapons, they had no choice. Blindfolded and cuffed, they were thrown into the car and taken away, to begin an ordeal, that, for John Cantlie at least, continues to this day.

Jim was praised by everyone he ever met as a gentle, caring man. In the darkened cells where he and others were held for almost twenty-one months, he lifted spirits when they were down, shared his meager bread when others were hungry, gave them blankets when they were cold. In the small cellars, he instigated games to keep other prisoners' minds sharp and to keep hope when there was little. They would talk about families and memories, and where they'd meet when they were released. They'd recite films from beginning to end, or give each other lectures on topics they knew. On some occasions, they found themselves laughing, even there in the darkest of dark places.

At the time ISIS, didn't yet exist as an entity, and they had been captured instead by Jabhat al-Nusra. Moved from prison to prison, it appears that they were shuttled between various groups as the factions morphed and split. When ISIS emerged, they must have been handed or sold on—ISIS had been amassing Western journalists, paying large money for them—knowing their real worth.

US journalist Peter Theo Curtis was also a prisoner of Jabhat al-Nusra around that time (though held separately), but was released following an intervention by the Qatari government. He wrote a first person account of the horrors they faced, and it makes for difficult reading.

Writing in the *New York Times*, Curtis described in detail the taunting, beating, and humiliation. The sense of hopelessness and of confusion he felt—unable to comprehend hope or how to rationalize his captivity. He was beaten so badly that he passed out for days, with sticks, fists, rope, feet—anything they could get. He was slammed against concrete walls, forced to stand for hours on end, blindfolded, and starved. For years, he slept curled in a ball on the cold concrete floor of his cell.

Sometimes they would put a tire around his legs to keep him still, turn him upside down, and whip his bare feet with a steel cable. This went on for years.

We know the prisoners went through a horrendous ordeal. Sometimes they were water-boarded while others watched. But in the hours and days between these torments, Jim made a pact with the other prisoners—that each would memorize a letter from the others, in case only one made it home.

Danish photographer Daniel Rye Ottosen was the one who made it out, and here is the letter written by Jim in that cell in Syria that Daniel memorized and took back to Jim's parents. They released it to the media after his death. These are his words:

Dear Family and Friends,

I remember going to the mall with Dad, a very long bike ride with Mom. I remember so many great family times that take me away from this prison. Dreams of family and friends take me away and happiness fills my heart.

I know you are thinking of me and praying for me. And I am so thankful. I feel you all especially when I pray. I pray for you to stay strong and to believe. I really feel I can touch you even in this darkness when I pray.

Eighteen of us have been held together in one cell, which has helped me. We have had each other to have endless long conversations about movies, trivia, sports. We have played games made up of scraps found in our cell...we have found ways to play checkers, Chess, and Risk... and have had tournaments of competition, spending some days preparing strategies for the next day's game or lecture. The games and teaching each other have helped the time pass. They have been a huge help. We repeat stories and laugh to break the tension.

I have had weak and strong days. We are so grateful when anyone is freed; but of course, yearn for our own freedom. We try to encourage each other and share strength. We are being fed better now and daily. We have tea, occasional coffee. I have regained most of my weight lost last year.

I think a lot about my brothers and sister. I remember playing Werewolf in the dark with Michael and so many other adventures. I think of chasing Mattie and T around the kitchen counter. It makes me happy to think of them. If there is any money left in my bank account, I want it to go to Michael and Matthew. I am so proud of you, Michael and thankful to you for happy childhood memories and to you and Kristie for happy adult ones.

And big John, how I enjoyed visiting you and Cress in Germany. Thank you for welcoming me. I think a lot about RoRo and try to imagine what Jack is like. I hope he has RoRo's personality!

And Mark... so proud of you too Bro. I think of you on the West coast and hope you are doing some snowboarding and camping, I especially remember us going to the Comedy Club in Boston together and our big hug after. The special moments keep me hopeful.

Katie, so very proud of you. You are the strongest and best of us all!! I think of you working so hard, helping people as a nurse. I am so glad we texted just before I was captured. I pray I can come to your wedding.... now I am sounding like Grammy!!

Grammy, please take your medicine, take walks and keep dancing. I plan to take you out to Margarita's when I get home. Stay strong because I am going to need your help to reclaim my life.

Jim

CHAPTER EIGHT

Sex

A scribbled note found in Anbar province, Iraq, lays bare the depravity and hypocrisy of ISIS. In it, the names of women are lined alongside those of fighters, together with the allotted time they will sleep with each—it is in effect a schedule of sex. The document is completely at odds with the supposed piety of the fighters, but they have found a way to justify it.

In the ISIS constitution, rule fourteen states, "Allah calls you to modesty, chastity, and loose-fitting gowns. Settling at home and staying in an honorable room, avoiding going out unless out of necessity, this is the way of the Mothers of the Believers and the dignified women companions." However, they consider non-Muslims to be apostate, and as the Yazidi religion pre-dates Islam, and does not follow a holy book, different rules apply to Yazidi women.

Sex is arranged for the fighters, both from girls who offer themselves, and, in many more cases, from girls whom they abduct. The document is entitled, "Schedule for Brothers, of Marriages with Mujahidaat" (female mujahideen), yet in it, each girl—Aishah, Marwa, and Om Umar—marries three times a day—and each marriage lasts for only two hours.

In 2013, a Saudi based cleric issued a fatwa, calling on woman to offer themselves to the armed fighters, as a way of joining the battle themselves in what is known as Nikka Jihad, or "Marriage jihad." Girls are known to have flocked from around the world into Syria including from the United States and the United Kingdom, to be shared among up to one hundred fighters, before returning, as a Tunisian minister said, "pregnant and bearing the fruit of sexual contacts in the name of sexual jihad."

They are able to justify this due to the two types of marriage within Islam. One, a permanent marriage as we all know it, the other, a fixed time marriage known as Mut'ah or Sigha—for which there is no minimum time. In the eyes of ISIS, if a women gives herself like this, it is considered a legitimate jihad—it's thought that the women, like the fighters, are making sacrifices—in their case, their chastity and dignity—in order to help the sexually frustrated jihadis focus on the war.

But there are so many other sickening stories coming out of ISIS territory where the women and girls have no choice. One resident of Mosul described to me how the marauding ISIS fighters scour cities for women to sleep with. In these cases they "marry" the girls for three days, keeping them captive, before divorcing them when they have finished raping them.

"They have arranged teams, who drive around knocking on doors," he told me. "They turn up heavily armed, with their black flags, demanding all the girls who are unmarried. Often the men are foreign; from Chechnya, Tunisia, and Afghanistan. They believe it is their right."

Going from house to house, they ask if the girls, some as young as fourteen, are married yet. If not, they are given twenty-four hours to find a husband or be "married" to the terrorists. In some cases, they use government records to find those who are unmarried before turning up on the doorstep with an Imam to marry them there and then. They have no choice.

To marry, the man must simply say, "I marry you" three times before then saying, " I divorce you," when he is done. Some families have tried to put up resistance. One father in Mosul waited in his house with a gun, before opening fire on ISIS fighters looking for a wife; he killed them before fleeing to the north with his family.

In another house, a girl heard them coming at night, waited with a gun, and opened fire herself, killing two before being shot. For most there is little to be done to save themselves, and to openly oppose ISIS leads to death, crucifixion, or decapitation.

Such is the dishonor felt by some of these girls, that many have committed suicide, while others have fled to camps in the north. It's from these crowded refugee camps that the stories are emerging.

Yazidi

In the vast refugee camp of Khanke, in northern Iraq, stories of ISIS brutality abound. Khanke is home to around fifteen thousand displaced Iraqis (small in comparison to the others), many of them Yazidis, and many of them missing family members. In the summer months, Khanke is a dry, barren desert and families sleep under open tents in the oppressive heat, crowding around the water pumps for their share of daily water. In winter, Khanke is cold, wet, and muddy, and water seeps into the belongings and tents of every refugee.

Many of the families in Khanke are missing their women or children—victims of sexual enslavement by ISIS—or missing their men—killed in cold blood. It is estimated that between five thousand and seven thousand mostly young girls have been taken from the villages around Mount Sinjar—traditionally the Yazidi heartland—and most of these have been raped and forced to marry older ISIS fighters.

ISIS brags about kidnapping and killing Yazidis, and considers them as prizes. One-fifth of the girls taken go to ISIS as a "tax," the rest are split among the fighters as a war prize. There is little doubt that their actions are genocidal—specifically targeting members of the Yazidi tribe.

When ISIS tore through Iraq, one of their priorities was the abolition of the Yazidis, and they slaughtered many of them. Most others fled to the large plain atop Mount Sinjar, where they were surrounded by ISIS troops. To get there, they walked for days, through hundred degree heat, with very little water or food. Many couldn't make it, and there were tragic stories of some families making the choice to abandon a baby to save the rest of their family.

As the refugees flocked to Mount Sinjar, a small battalion of Kurdish troops tried to protect the thirty thousand refugees, but in the face of the ISIS onslaught, there was not much they could do. The Yazidis were pushed further along the thirty mile inhospitable mountaintop, until they were cornered. Only then, at the last minute, did the United States intervene, sending planes to save those who remained, and supporting the delivery of food and water.

The battle for Mount Sinjar further galvanized public opinion and shone a light on ISIS's ethnic cleansing. In the eyes of ISIS, Yazidis are devil worshipers, and their slaughter is encouraged. Yazidis are predominantly Kurdish by ethnicity, and are one of the oldest religions in the region—taking much of their teaching from Zoroastrianism. Their religion is transferred by word of mouth—in fact, it predates all "holy texts." ISIS sees any religion that doesn't have a Bible or Koran as satanic, and so they genuinely believe that they should be enslaved or killed.

Even Christians are given more opportunities, and, if lucky, are allowed to escape by paying a tax. The Yazidis have no such chance, and at one point a vast number of the total eight hundred thousand Yazidis in the world were threatened with death. Certainly the oldest Yazidi settlement—in the plains of Ninevah—is now almost void of Yazidis.

Renda's Story

Stories of the ISIS attacks on Yazidis in August 2014, and the subsequent abuse of their girls, have been slowly reaching the outside world, either via those who have escaped or those who have been sold back to their families—and these stories are sickening. In the camps like Khanke and Dohuk, there are so many brutal tales that it's hard to know which one to tell, and I wish I could tell them all. But here is one I've heard, one like many others. This is Renda's story.

Renda was one of the many girls who was caught while fleeing her village and who has lost most of her family. I've called her Renda but this isn't her real name. She is both too embarrassed and scared to use it, fearful that it might endanger the remaining members of her family still alive under ISIS rule, and terrified that it will bring shame on her family. She's sixteen years old.

In mid August, hearing that ISIS fighters were approaching her village, and having heard about what would happen if they were caught, Renda and her family (her parents, younger sister, and older brother) fled north towards Mount Sinjar. They had packed just a small bag each, with some clothes and some photos. They rushed into the family car and left with a group of others, heading across the barren landscape in convoy. As they sped along in their old car, they saw a convoy of powerful ISIS trucks appear in the distance behind them—trucks that slowly began to gain on them.

Her father tried to outrun them, but it was useless. Renda described the car bouncing around on the dirt road, knocking them around the car and onto the ceiling. Renda and her sisters were screaming as ISIS pulled ever closer, watching out of the back window as the trucks caught up with them. She remembers seeing the fighters screaming in the trucks and pointing at them. Finally, the fighters pulled in front of their car, leapt out, and stopped them. They were caught.

They were grabbed out of the cars and lined up along

the desert road. The ISIS fighters separated them first by religion—allowing the Sunnis to continue on their way, and keeping the Yazidis there. Then they split them by age and sex. The young women and girls were put to the side in one group, fighting age men in an another, and the elderly in a third. The girls were loaded into a truck, the elderly were allowed to continue, and the men were shot.

Renda was driven away with her sister, knowing that her father and brother had been killed, and her mother was now alone. Her whole life was about to change. They were taken towards the Syrian border where they were placed in a building with countless other girls. Renda never knew how many others, as they were kept in various rooms, but by speaking to the others she knew that there were corridors full of rooms, each with around twenty girls in it. It sounds likely that at one point, she was held at Badoush prison in Mosul.

She was taken to a few different buildings—never sure why she was being moved or where she was going. Each time she was moved she met new girls, and they tried to stick together and console each other. She talked about how they would hug each other at night, and how they would try to calm the younger girls. Sometimes the fighters would give them mobile phones and tell them to call their families, and tell them what was happening to them. There are stories of girls being raped while speaking to their parents.

Sometimes they'd be locked up for days straight, and not allowed to leave the cell. Everywhere Renda was taken, she heard girls being raped in the rooms around her. They would be taken out randomly and brought back later, often beaten and crying. Girls were passed among groups of men, and beaten if they resisted—punched and kicked. They would be placed in the middle of circles, busy rooms full of fighters who would laugh and spit on them as they huddled in the middle. Men would barter among themselves to see which ones they would have, and which ones they would marry.

Renda denies being raped herself, saying she resisted. This is common to hear among the girls who have been released or who have escaped. They talk in detail about the rape of other girls but deny they were raped themselves; such is the shame on them and their families that very few can admit to it. She admits to considering suicide, and indeed there are many girls who took their own lives.

The girls were terrified all the time, usually fed just once a day, and often taunted by the fighters, who seemed to take it as a game. Renda was at a few of these busy "markets" until one day she was bought by an older man, who she believed was a leader of some sort. After this she was moved into Syria with two other girls. She was kept for a few weeks at a large house in the countryside, and beaten repeatedly. She says she didn't marry the old man as others were forced to do, but she seems to have been kept as a slave. Again she denies being raped.

After some weeks, she was given a chance to escape—the house was not so guarded, and she was allowed to move around a bit and go to the toilet. Late one night, she crept out of a window with one other girl, and they ran across the fields. Terrified, and with no idea where she was, she took a chance and knocked on the door of a farm building about an hour away. The man who took her in was not so kind, but agreed to help. They called the family of the other girl, and began to arrange their freedom.

It was still a couple of weeks before they left, and it seems that this was until the families were able to raise the money that the man requested. I don't know how much, but I've heard figures of anywhere from three thousand dollars to fifteen thousand dollars to smuggle girls back. One day, they put on niqabs, the head to toe Muslim clothing favored in the region, and set off. Near the border, they were swapped into other cars and handed to smugglers, who ferried them back to Iraq. Renda was finally reunited with her mother, and today they are rebuilding their lives, but with all the men in their family dead, Renda's sister still missing, and no home to speak of, they have little except each other.

There are go-betweens, who arrange for the families to buy back the girls, and a few hundred have been recovered this way, but despite looking, as more time passes, it becomes harder and harder to find the remaining girls.

ISIS openly documents its own disgusting treatment of women, specifically Yazidi women, of whom an estimated twenty-seven hundred have been taken. Writing in an edition of their magazine, Dabiq, they justify their actions in an article entitled "The Revival of Slavery Before the Hour" ("Hour" referring to Judgment Day).

"Before Satan reveals his doubts to the weak-minded and weak hearted, one should remember that enslaving the families of the kuffar (infidels) and taking their women as concubines, is a firmly established aspect of the Shari'ah, that if one were to deny or mock, he would be denying or mocking the verses of the Qur'an and the narration of the Prophet ...."

The stories of abuse are sickening, and in many cases come from the victims themselves, who are forced to call their parents and recount their repeated rape. Once they are captured, the women are split into groups based on age and religion before being sent to the markets for sale. They can fetch anything from twenty-five dollars to one thousand dollars, based on eye color, looks, and age.

The magazine goes on to explain: "After capture, the Yazidi women and children were then divided according to the Shari'ah amongst the fighters of the Islamic State who participated in the Sinjar operations, after one-fifth of the slaves were transferred to the Islamic State's authority to be divided as khums." Khums are the portion of all war spoils that jihadi fighters must pay to the caliph—always one fifth of what they have caught—the rest is split between the men.

The girls are offered the chance to convert—and if they do, are sold as wives. If not, they are kept under guard in small rooms and raped by countless fighters. Some have described rooms of hell, where they are brought to be used by one fighter after another. The stories are foul, and many girls speak of wishing they were dead. "They have killed my body, they are now killing my soul," one told Pakhshan Zangana, head of the High Council of Women's Affairs, a group that tries to buy the girls back before they disappear. "They all beat us but I wish they would beat us till we were dead."

In a sickening cell phone video released online, fighters are seen in a busy room, relaxing, laughing, and joking about the upcoming sale of women and about how much they will pay—it's the fighters pay day.

"Today is the slave market day," one grins at the camera.

"Where is my Yazidi girl?" another shouts, laughing. "I am looking for one. Who wants to sell their girl to me?"

"I do," another cries. "I'll sell her for a pistol."

"I'll give you three hundred dollars—but the price is better if she's got blue eyes. If she's fifteen, I'll have to check her—check her teeth."

A young boy looks up at the camera. "Do you want a Yazidi too?" He giggles and nods. "Would you know what to do with her?"

They all laugh.

Another video shows the stoning of a woman in front of her father, who refuses to forgive her for adultery. In the heartrending film, the ISIS fighter tells the girl, "No one forced you, so you need to accept God's law, and to accept, and submit to God. Islam is submitting to the will of God." She accepts the punishment before turning to her father and begging him for forgiveness, her voice quivering and crying. He refuses, saying, "My heart doesn't obey me, I can't forgive you." And the girl is then bound together and led by her father to a hole in the ground, where she will stand until being stoned. The video cuts to her limp body surrounded by stones.

Treatment of Slaves

In October of 2014, ISIS published a document to justify its abuse of women, and set guidelines for what can and can't be done to them. It isn't easy reading, but must be read by all.

"Question 1: What is al-sabi?"

"Al-Sabi is a woman from among who has been captured by Muslims."

"Question 2: What makes al-sabi permissible?"

"What makes al-sabi permissible [i.e., what makes it permissible to take such a woman captive] is [her] unbelief. Unbelieving [women] who were captured and brought into the abode of Islam are permissible to us, after the imam distributes them [among us]."

"Question 3: Can all unbelieving women be taken captive?"

"There is no dispute among the scholars that it is permissible to capture unbelieving women [who are characterized by] original unbelief [kufr asli], such as the kitabiyat [women from among the People of the

Book, i.e. Jews and Christians] and polytheists. However, [the scholars] are disputed over [the issue of] capturing apostate women. The consensus leans towards
forbidding it, though some people of knowledge think
it permissible. We [ISIS] lean towards accepting the
consensus..."

"Question 4: Is it permissible to have intercourse
with a female captive?"

"It is permissible to have sexual intercourse with
the female captive. Allah the almighty said: '[Success-
ful are the believers] who guard their chastity, except
from their wives or (the captives and slaves) that their
right hands possess, for then they are free from blame
[Koran 23:5-6]'..."

"Question 5: Is it permissible to have intercourse with
a female captive immediately after taking possession
[of her]?"

"If she is a virgin, he [her master] can have intercourse with her immediately after taking possession of
her. However, if she isn't, her uterus must be purified
[first]..."

"Question 6: Is it permissible to sell a female captive?"

"It is permissible to buy, sell, or give as a gift female
captives and slaves, for they are merely property, which

can be disposed of [as long as that doesn't cause [the Muslim ummah] any harm or damage."

"Question 7: Is it permissible to separate a mother from her children through [the act of] buying and selling?"

"It is not permissible to separate a mother from her prepubescent children through buying, selling or giving away [a captive or slave]. [But] it is permissible to separate them if the children are grown and mature."

"Question 8: If two or more [men] buy a female captive together, does she then become [sexually] permissible to each of them?"

"It is forbidden to have intercourse with a female captive if [the master] does not own her exclusively. One who owns [a captive] in partnership [with others] may not have sexual intercourse with her until the other [owners] sell or give him [their share]."

"Question 9: If the female captive was impregnated by her owner, can he then sell her?"

"He can't sell her if she becomes the mother of a child..."

"Question 10: If a man dies, what is the law regarding the female captive he owned?"

"Female captives are distributed as part of his estate, just as all [other parts] of his estate [are distributed]. However, they may only provide services, not intercourse, if a father or [one of the] sons has already had intercourse with them, or if several [people] inherit them in partnership."

"Question 11: May a man have intercourse with the female slave of his wife?"

"A man may not have intercourse with the female slave of his wife, because [the slave] is owned by someone else."

"Question 12: May a man kiss the female slave of another, with the owner's permission?"

"A man may not kiss the female slave of another, for kissing [involves] pleasure, and pleasure is prohibited unless [the man] owns [the slave] exclusively."

"Question 13: Is it permissible to have intercourse with a female slave who has not reached puberty?"

"It is permissible to have intercourse with the female slave who hasn't reached puberty if she is fit for inter course; however if she is not fit for intercourse, then it is enough to enjoy her without intercourse."

"Question 14: What private parts of the female slave's body must be concealed during prayer?"

"Her private body parts [that must be concealed] during prayer are the same as those [that must be concealed] outside [prayer], and they [include] everything besides the head, neck, hands and feet."

"Question 15: May a female slave meet foreign men without wearing a hijab?"

"A female slave is allowed to expose her head, neck, hands, and feet in front of foreign men if fitna [enticement] can be avoided. However, if fitna is present, or of there is fear that it will occur, then it [i.e. exposing these body parts] is forbidden."

"Question 16: Can two sisters be taken together while taking slaves?"

"It is permissible to have two sisters, a female slave and her aunt [her father's sister], or a female slave and her aunt [from her mother's side]. But they cannot be together during intercourse, [and] whoever has intercourse with one of them cannot have intercourse with the other, due to the general [consensus] over the prohibition of this."

"Question 17: What is al-'azl?"

"Al-'azl is refraining from ejaculating on a woman's pudendum [i.e. coitus interruptus]."

"Question 18: May a man use the al-'azl [technique] with his female slave?"

"A man is allowed [to use] al-'azl during intercourse with his female slave with or without her consent."

"Question 19: Is it permissible to beat a female slave?"

"It is permissible to beat the female slave as a [form of] darb ta'deeb [disciplinary beating], [but] it is forbidden to [use] darb al-takseer [literally, breaking beating], [darb] al-tashaffi [beating for the purpose of achieving gratification], or [darb] al-ta'dheeb [torture beating]. Further, it is forbidden to hit the face."

"Question 20: What is the ruling regarding a female slave who runs away from her master?"

"A male or female slave's running away [from their master] is among the gravest of sins..."

"Question 21: What is the earthly punishment of a female slave who runs away from her master?"

"She [i.e. the female slave who runs away from her master] has no punishment according to the shari'a of Allah; however, she is [to be] reprimanded [in such a way that] deters others like her from escaping."

"Question 22: Is it permissible to marry a Muslim [slave] or a kitabiyya [i.e. Jewish or Christian] female slave?"

"It is impermissible for a free [man] to marry Muslim or kitabiyat female slaves, except for those [men] who feared to [commit] a sin, that is, the sin of fornication…"

"Question 23: If a man marries a female slave who is owned by someone else, who is allowed to have intercourse with her?"

"A master is prohibited from having intercourse with his female slave who is married to someone else; instead, the master receives her service, [while] the husband [gets to] enjoy her [sexually]."

"Question 24: Are the huddoud [Koranic punishments] applied to female slaves?"

"If a female slave committed what necessitated the enforcement of a hadd [on her], a hadd [is then] enforced on her – however, the hadd is reduced by half within the hudud that accepts reduction by half…"

"Question 25: What is the reward for freeing a slave girl?"

"Allah the exalted said [in the Koran]: 'And what can make you know what is [breaking through] the difficult pass [hell]? It is the freeing of a slave.' And [the prophet Muhammad] said: 'Whoever frees a believer Allah frees every organ of his body from hellfire.'"

Translation Courtesy of MEMRI
Middle East Media Research Institute

© Photo by REX

Steven Sotloff, journalist, murdered by ISIS, August 4, 2014

CHAPTER NINE

Steven Sotloff

Steven, thirty-one years old, was born in Pinecrest, Florida. By his own admission, he was a self-appointed "stand-up philosopher from Miami," and he always made others smile. He enjoyed South Park, junk food, and American football, but he was also a dedicated war photographer who had traveled and lived in the region for some years, covering countries from Yemen to Libya to Lebanon, where he lived. His mother paid tribute to him following his death, saying, "He had a gentle soul that this world will be without, but his spirit will endure in our hearts."

He was captured close to the Turkish border soon after crossing, by a group of men who had set up a fake checkpoint. The border crossing at Kilis is a veritable highway and groups from all sides have it watched. The hotels in Kilis are used as staging grounds for cross border trips, and are also well known, and journalists hanging around are liable to be spotted and possibly tracked. If it wasn't in Kilis that Steven was spotted, then it was certainly as he crossed in early August, 2013.

His captors knew he was coming, and were waiting for him on the road to Aleppo. Barak Barfi, a friend of Steven's and a spokesman for his family, has said that moderate rebels sold details of his crossing to ISIS, for something between twenty-five and fifty thousand dollars.

He was moved into Aleppo, and held in a few places before being transferred to the same cell as other hostages. During captivity, while others converted to Islam in the hope that it would save them, Steven remained true to his Jewish faith. According to a witness, he even went as far as to fake an illness on Yom Kippur, as an excuse to refuse food and observe the fast.

Some time before he was beheaded on September 2, 2014, Steven was also able to smuggle out a letter for his parents, from which his aunt read at his funeral:

"Please know I'm OK. Live your life to the fullest and fight to be happy. Everyone has two lives. The second one begins when you realize you only have one. I hope to see you soon. Stay positive and patient. If we are not together again, perhaps God will reunite us in Heaven."

Rescue Operation

On July 4, 2014, Special Forces launched a rescue attempt for the remaining hostages. Sometime in the spring, they had been moved towards the ISIS capital of Raqqa, and the threat against them was seen as growing.

Under the cover of darkness, a heavily-armed and modified Black Hawk helicopter from the regiment known as the Night Stalkers swooped on a compound near Raqqa known as "Osama bin Laden Camp." Two dozen US commandos, parachuted in, supported by fixed-wing planes and helicopters, and simultaneously blocked the road to Raqqa, and launched an attack on the compound. As an unknown number of ISIS fighters arrived from Raqqa, they were engaged and a three hour firefight ensued. One Special Forces soldier was wounded, and approximately five ISIS fighters were killed. RPG's were fired at the helicopters overhead, though with scant success. Little else is known about what happened that night, but the rescue attempt failed—and none of the hostages were present. It's thought that they had been moved to a series of tunnels underneath the city of Raqqa.

Over time, the number of hostages being held by ISIS in Raqqa had diminished as they had been ransomed and released. It had become clear to the prisoners such releases were determined by the passports they held. When David Haines was kept, while his European co-worker with whom he'd been kidnapped was released, the situation became dire.

In their English language magazine Dabiq, ISIS wrote, "As the American government was dragging its feet, reluctant to save James Foley's life, negotiations were made by the governments of a number of European prisoners, which resulted in the release of a dozen of their prisoners after the demands of the Islamic State were met."

Intelligence must have shown that with the continuing refusal of the United States and United Kingdom to pay ransoms, time was running out. There are many who say the raid was too little too late, and that having debriefed the previously released hostages, they could have acted sooner. *Global Posts*'s President and Chief Executive, Philip Balboni, for whom Jim Foley had worked, for and who spent millions of dollars trying to secure his release, said, "We knew exactly where he was from the released hostages."

Details of this raid were only declassified after the death of Jim Foley.

CHAPTER TEN

A Cold War:
Saudi Arabia vs Iran

To fully understand the Syrian conflict, where it came from, and the conditions that led to the rise of ISIS, we have to look at the puppeteers pulling the strings. No two stand out more than Saudi Arabia and Iran. Ultimately, this is an age-old battle fought between two enemies, both set on each other's destruction; it is a story of intrigue, espionage, and manipulation. On the surface, it's about religion, but yet again we see that it is merely used as an excuse to galvanize their respective populations. In reality it's about power, and the ability of each country to exert influence over the region.

There are two men who best personify this proxy war between Saudi Arabia and Iran, which is at the core of the ideological split within the Middle East. One is the ebullient Saudi Prince Bandar bin Sultan, former ambassador spectacular to a succession of US presidents, and until recently head of Saudi intelligence services. The other is General Qassem Suleimani, shadowy head of Iran's notorious Quds force—a branch of Iran's Revolutionary Guard, responsible for covert overseas operations.

These two men had both been at the vanguard of the Syrian conflict, yet in August of 2014, Bandar was replaced as Saudi intelligence chief, a clear sign that King Abdullah was displeased with his policies and that Saudi policy had backfired. At the same time, Suleimani was being praised as "a living hero" by Ayatollah Ali Khamenei, and for the first time, pictures of him began to circulate widely in Iranian media. But what brought about these changes?

Initially, Prince Bandar's Saudi policy had been to fund all Sunni opposition in Syria. He believed that Assad would fall quickly as with other Arab Spring dictators, and that Saudi Arabia could spend their way to a victory over Iran. It didn't initially matter that some hardliners were receiving funding, as they believed they could rein them in later.

Former Saudi intelligence director Prince Turki al-Faisal once said, "We don't do operations, and we don't know how. All we know how to do is write checks." It appears that in this case, the policy didn't work, and henceforth Saudi became an unwitting player in the growth of ISIS.

Suleimani, on the other hand, has been instrumental in organizing the successful involvement of Hezbollah to defend Assad and Baghdad, and has often been seen in Damascus and Baghdad, organizing their defenses. He is said to be behind the strategy to make Assad appear a lesser threat than ISIS, and indeed, it wasn't long after the emergence of ISIS that the United States started quietly working alongside Assad, providing him with the locations of ISIS targets for use in air strikes, a major coup for Suleimani! Turkey, along with Saudi Arabia and other Gulf states, have been furious to see US priority move away from the removal of Assad, and as a result embarked on a more unilateral approach.

Prince Bandar

© Photo by Mark Reinstein/REX

Prince Bandar bin Sultan. Long serving Saudi Ambassador to the US, intelligence chief, and initial architect of Saudi Arabia's policy in Syria.

The respective characters of Bandar and Suleimani perfectly represent their countries' approaches to foreign policy. Bandar is the globe-trotting billionaire, close friends with US presidents and son of the late crown prince Sultan bin Abdulaziz al-Saud. He smokes large cigars, wears well-tailored suits, and has arranged some of the biggest arms deals in history. He attends regular Dallas Cowboy games, sitting next to the owner, builds libraries, and has been known as the "King's exclusive messenger, and the White House's errand boy." For over three decades, he was the face of the Saudi Arabia lobby in the United States. He has orchestrated the creation of Sunni militias in Lebanon, and advised on the support of Sunni groups in Syria. He is ultimately considered a charming man by those in the West, and "The Prince of Terrorists" in Iran. He embodies perfectly the close historical relationship between Saudi Arabia and the United States.

General Suleimani

© Photo by AY-Collection/Sipa/REX

Qassem Suleimani, Head of Iran's Quds force, the unit responsible for operations abroad. He is the architect of Iran's policy in Syria.

Suleimani, on the other hand, was born in Rabor, a poor mountain village in eastern Iran, and as a boy worked as a laborer to clear family debts. He had just completed high school when the Iranian Revolution began, and he joined the republican guard. He spent his childhood listening to sermons by visiting Shia preachers, and went on to fight in many battles, and was wounded many times before working his way up to head of the Quds force. He lives a modest life in Tehran, has an office in the old United States embassy compound, wakes up at 4 a.m., and is said to suffer from a bad back. Today, as one former CIA agent has said, "He is the single most powerful operative in the Middle East—and no one's ever heard of him." He has arranged covert attacks everywhere from Thailand to Nairobi, and in 2011 hired a Mexican cartel to blow up the Saudi ambassador to the United States (Bandar's successor). The plot failed, as the gang member was an undercover DEA agent. Early in the United States, war against the Taliban, he was instrumental in sharing information with the US defense department, a brief collaboration that would end suddenly with Iran's inclusion in the axis of evil.

These two characters define their countries respective foreign policies, but first it's crucial to understand what's at the heart of Saudi-Iranian enmity. Ultimately, at its very core ISIS was born from the age-old ideological battle between the two, and the religious struggle for supremacy between Sunni and Shia. I won't go into the differences between Sunni and Shia, but to put it briefly, Sunnis consider Shiites heretics, much as the Catholics did Protestants during the reformation and now, as back then, we are seeing unmentionable acts done in Gods' name.

Historical Differences

To understand the actions of Saudi Arabia and Iran over the last few decades, imagine it as a cold war. Technically, both countries are at peace, but the countries between them function as a highly volatile chess board. All of the countries have both Sunni and Shia populations, (though the majority are Sunni) and a few in the middle have significant populations of each—Iraq, Syria, Lebanon, Bahrain.

The shifting spheres of influence at the end of the twentieth century though, have brought this simmering conflict to the boil. After the fall of Saddam in 2003, Iran successfully took control of the Iraqi government (Iraq being sixty to seventy percent Shia) and expanded its control across the region, effectively controlling an arc of influence all the way from Tehran to Hezbollah in Lebanon, via Damascus and Baghdad. In doing so, they seriously encroached on Saudi hegemony.

When the United States removed the Taliban from Afghanistan—also long-term enemies of Iran but allies of Saudi Arabia—another blow was dealt to Saudi influence, and Iran began vying for more power. In light of cooling relations between the United States and Saudi Arabia under the Obama administration, which were once the bedrock of policy in the region, Saudi Arabia felt it had no choice but to launch a far more aggressive foreign policy on its own, and take care of its interests single-handedly.

So when the opportunity arose for Saudi Arabia to push back Iranian influence by supporting the fight against Allawite Assad, they took matters into their own hands.

Yes, the Syrian revolution began as a nascent rebel movement, an uprising of people against an oppressive regime, but it was soon hijacked. Saudi Arabia put their weight behind Sunni groups who could sway the balance of power, and quickly allowed weapons and funding to flow to them.

They believed that they could control these forces as they had done for decades with the Wahhabis back home, but eventually that turned out to be false. Ultimately, there is a fine line between jihadists and Islamists, and a very large grey area in between—this grey area was swept up by jihad.

As ISIS continued to grow and spread, they started to pose an ever more serious domestic threat to the House of Saud, which has long had an uneasy relationship with its religious core. Saudi Arabia has its domestic security to worry about, and as it watched more and more if its citizens flocking to fight in Syria, it became increasingly concerned about returning fighters seeking to destabilize Riyahd. As ISIS moved ever closer to the Jordanian border, this became an increasing threat.

Saudi Arabia also underestimated the support Assad would get from Iran and Russia, and the resistance they would put up, so the more ISIS grew, the more it became clear that Bandar's plans had backfired.

Balancing Act

This balancing act by Saudi Arabia—the creation and support of jihadists abroad in an attempt to influence regional affairs—is by no means new. Its funding of conflicts elsewhere has long been used to divert jihadists away from home, and what better way to achieve this than by encouraging them to fight in places like Bosnia, Chechnya, or Afghanistan? In fact, support of Sunni jihad has long been the foundation of Saudi policy, and one which has kept them in favor with the Wahhabi clerics they tolerate. In 2009, a cable released by Wikileaks showed that Saudi Arabia, while cracking down on Al-Qaeda activities domestically, had done nothing to prevent them abroad.

Puritanical Wahhabism in Saudi Arabia runs to the core of society, though for many decades the house of Saud managed to placate them. The beliefs of Wahabiism are very similar to those of Al-Qaeda, and the country is often seen as home to the global jihadist movement. By supporting their mosques, schools, and clerics, the establishment persuaded them to turn a blind eye to their own extravagances, as well as their close relationship with the United States.

In supporting fundamentalists in Syria (not necessarily ISIS, but its precursors) Saudi Arabia would be able to serve two goals—a strike against Iran, and a chance to highlight its credentials as defender of Islam, and keep its restive population appeased.

What they could not foresee was that ISIS would grow so strong. On realizing this, they began to reevaluate their support for the most hard-line fighters—though many would say too late. Saudi Arabia was blinded by their struggle with Iran for so long, that they lost control of the force they set out to create, and have ultimately created a monster they can no longer predict.

Saudi King Abdullah Bin Abdulaziz, finally addressed the United Nations using the most persuasive angle he could think of: "If neglected I'm sure they [ISIS] will reach Europe in a month and America in another month... The evils of terrorism must be fought with force, reason and speed." Yet despite all this—they must still be held to account.

Iran

Meanwhile, Iran has been stoking the sectarian flames as well, and is as much to blame for the creation of ISIS as Saudi Arabia. Ultimately, they have been prepared to go to any lengths to protect their interests in Syria, and in doing so shore up Assad's murderous regime, resupplying his armories by air over Iraq, and allowing him to continue the mass slaughter of his people has only galvanized hatred against Iran.

That Iran would rather stoke a brutal civil war against the civilians of Syria in order to keep control of Damascus, than replace Assad with someone who could start a transitional government, is a sign of how important Damascus is to them.

Ultimately, control of southern Syria provides crucial access to their Lebanon proxy Hezbollah, allowing them to pass on weapons and money. It also acts as a deterrent against Israel from attacking Iran's nuclear program and proxies, and is the bedrock of their regional influence.

It's because of Iran's continued support for Assad that the war has escalated, and it's a result of the heinous crimes committed that Sunnis flock from around the world to join the fight. And there were so many jihadists looking for battle. After the end of the wars in Iraq and Afghanistan, battle hardened fighters were itching for another battle. From Mali to Libya there is now a roving network of fighters fighting under the banner of Islam, and that ideological war is taking hold in minds around the world.

But Iran is also guilty of encouraging Maliki to consolidate power in Iraq, and is responsible for the failure of democracy to take hold. So when Obama sought to improve relations with Iran, he was ignoring Iran's role in all the regions' conflicts—the stoking of sectarianism and the supporting of Assad's regime. Some commentators have pointed out that Iran excels at creating problems that only it is in a position to solve, and the regular sight of Suleimani, in Baghdad and Damascus points to the hand they have in this war.

The reason it is so important to speak about Saudi Arabia and Iran today, even though ISIS has a mind of its own, is because that only through pressing each side can we hope to solve this problem. Iran has to tell Assad to pull back, and replace him with someone more suited to lead negotiations, and Saudi Arabia has to stop stoking the violence and allowing funds and fighters to go there. This is to ask two age-old enemies to back down from each other, which will sadly never happen. Perhaps if the leadership of Iran was to fall, we might be able to work with the Iranian people, who are at the core more suitable partners for the West.

Even though one of ISIS's stated goals is to abolish the house of Saud, that would be very hard for them to achieve. They would first have to succeed in Syria and Iraq before they were able to launch any serious attack on Saudi Arabia, and even if that were to happen Saudi Arabia has the most powerful army in the region, one that is more than capable of holding them back. So, in many ways, they do more good for Saudi Arabia than bad. They may have lost control over their proxies, but Saudi Arabia is not really at threat. Nor is it really threatened by Shia Islam—only four of fifty-seven Muslim countries in the world have a Shia majority—yet that does not stop them from acting drastically when threatened in any small way. Look at how they cracked down on the Bahraini uprising in 2011, when they crushed the Shia majority.

Iran Created ISIS?

There is one other hypothesis, which should be mentioned. It suggests that Iran is responsible for the rise of ISIS; certainly, they have benefited from it in many ways: The pressure to remove their ally Assad from power has ceased, Iran is able to ally with the West in fighting ISIS, therefore acting as savior, and the West gets mired in another Middle Eastern conflict.

Many Syrian rebels I spoke to throughout 2013 and 2014 noted that Assad's Iranian backed air force focused its aerial bombardment on moderate FSA battalions, but rarely seemed to attack ISIS. At the same time, the Syrian regime is known to have bought back oil from wells under the control of ISIS, and in doing so filled the coffers of their feared enemy.

As ISIS became stronger, thanks in part to these actions, they also took over the mantle of public enemy number one, removing a lot of the pressure on Assad. We only have to look at how the press reports on the conflict between rebel forces and Assad drastically dropped after June 2014 to see that the battle against him has been largely forgotten. Instead, the focus has shifted to attacking the global jihadi threat, and, in doing so, the West found themselves strangely allied to him. There has been considerable communication between the United States and Assad, not least about using Syrian airspace to attack ISIS, something that would have been far more complicated with Syria's Russian made SA80 air defense system in play.

As well as taking the pressure off Assad, Iran also gained favor by offering its support to the United States. Since early 2012, the Iranians backed Kurdish troops in the north, protected Baghdad in the south and, as in the town of Amerli, actively fought alongside US forces against ISIS (the US Air Force provided air support while Iranian troops fought on ground).

Some people have noted that ISIS also arose at a time that nuclear negotiations were underway between Iran and the United States, and have speculated that if Iran can show its credentials in fighting ISIS, it might get leeway, from a US government that they see as weak and lacking in moral fiber—not being willing to see the war in Baghdad through to it's conclusion.

So, in one sense, Iran has ultimately benefited most from the rise of ISIS. They may not have minded losing northern Syria as long as they kept Baghdad and Damascus, but if they lost those, they would lose Hezbollah and their ability to project influence around Israel.

Now if you were to ask me whether it's possible for the United States and Iran to ally in the future, I would put it like this. In Saudi Arabia, we have a blackened core of Wahhabis and clerics whose very existence is based on wiping out the infidels. But we have a leadership allied with us, keeping them at bay, for our sakes, but mainly for theirs. But in Iran, we have the opposite: a leadership that is blackened, manipulates events around the globe, supports dictators like Assad, and subjugates its people. However, they control what is really a very pro-Western populous. I've been to Iran on a number of occasions, and the people overwhelmingly love the United States. They're welcoming and pragmatic, and they want freedom. Most importantly Shia Islam does not preach global jihad the way that Sunnis do. Our enemy in Iran is the state, not the people.

Alan Henning, Aid worker, murdered by ISIS, October 3, 2014

CHAPTER ELEVEN

Alan Henning and David Haines

"Alan is a peaceful, selfless man who left his family and his job as a taxi driver in the United Kingdom to drive in a convoy all the way to Syria with his Muslim colleagues and friends to help those most in need.

"When he was taken he was driving an ambulance full of food and water to be handed out to anyone in need. I cannot see how it could assist any state's cause to allow the world to see a man like Alan dying.

"I have been trying to communicate with the Islamic State and the people holding Alan. I have sent some really important messages but they have not been responded to. I pray that the people holding Alan respond to my messages and contact me before it is too late. When they hear this message I implore the people of Islamic State to see it in their hearts to release my husband Alan Henning."

—Barbara Henning, wife of Alan Henning

On Boxing Day in 2013, half an hour after crossing

into Syria, Henning was taken while unloading aid packages at a warehouse in the town Al-Dana. It's not known whether his captors were tipped off. Tragically, he spent the first part of his captivity in good humor, and according to a Syrian man held alongside him, he was sure he would be released when they learned he was an aid worker. But on October 3, 2014, he suffered the same fate as the others—he was brutally murdered after being force to read a statement.

"I'm Alan Henning. Because of our parliament's decision to attack the Islamic state I, as a member of the British public, will now pay the price for that decision."

David Haines

Haines, forty-four, was kidnapped in Atme in March 2013 while working for the French humanitarian aid agency ACTED. He'd spent many years working in humanitarian aid, helping victims of the conflicts in the former Yugoslavia and Sudan. Like many of the others who were taken, Haines was abducted while driving though the countryside returning from Aleppo. A car pulled up alongside them and shot out their tires, and masked men leapt out, surrounded the car, and grabbed them. They seemed to know there were Westerners inside. Haines had been in Syria for just three days when was taken by the rebel group, who later sold him to ISIS.

They seized him and his Italian co-worker, Mr. Motka, put them in the trunk of the car, and left the two Syrians by the road as they described the scene later. It was over in seconds. Haines leaves behind a four-year-old and a seventeen-year-old daughter.

In the video, before he is murdered, he gives this message:

"This British man has to pay the price for your promise, Cameron, to arm the peshmerga against the Islamic State. Ironically, he has spent a decade of his life serving under the same Royal Air Force responsible for delivering those arms. Your evil alliance with America which continues to strike the Muslims of Iraq and most recently bombed the Haditha Dam, will only accelerate your destruction, and playing the role of the obedient lapdog, Cameron, will only draw you and your people into another bloody and un-winnable war."

CHAPTER TWELVE

Qatar, Libya, Kuwait

Qatar

"Qatar can only follow a foreign policy that is independent of outside influence, and this is something we are proud of."
—Sheikh Al-Thani

Saudi Arabia and Iran are not the only countries to blame for the rapid escalation of jihadis in Syria; indeed the Saudi government, due to the threat of destabilization at home, has started to worry a lot more about the growing threat. However, Qatar, with a far less diverse populace, and a different outlook on the region's future, has been far less motivated.

Unlike Saudi Arabia, Qatar has not been so quick to crack down on the flow of money to ISIS and its motives in the region remain oblique. One theory suggests that doing so fits in with their foreign policy goals, and this puts them rather at odds with the United States. It also puts them at odds with other countries in the region, to such an extent that in March of 2014, Saudi Arabia, Bahrain, and the United Arab Emirates all withdrew their ambassadors from Qatar.

Over the last decade, Qatar has aggressively sought to become a new world power, investing vast sums of its almost unlimited wealth in everything from culture to media, Western corporations, football teams, and political sponsorship. As such, middlemen from all over the world's troubled spots have flocked to Doha seeking handouts: Hamas leader Khaled Meshaal, Darfuri rebels, Taliban leaders, ex-Saddam generals now fighting with ISIS, and Syrian opposition leaders have all used the country's glitzy hotels as a base.

Many extremist organizations also have close relationships with Qatar's government. It was Qatar who played middleman in the deal to get back US journalist Peter Theo Curtis from the al-Nusra front. It was Qatar who paid the twenty million dollar ransom for the release of forty-five abducted Fiji soldiers in the Golan Heights. And it was Qatar that brokered the controversial US prisoner swap with the Taliban to release Sergeant Bowe Bergdahl in exchange for five ranking Taliban members. The Taliban even have an embassy in Doha.

There are also numerous links between the Qatari royal family and Al-Qaeda. Bin Laden was known to a be a guest of the royal family on numerous occasions, receiving a warm welcome. Khaled Sheikh Mohammed, 9/11 mastermind, lived on a farm belonging to Qatar's minister of religious affairs, Abdallah bin

Khalid al-Thani. Al-Thani paid for him to fight in Bosnia, and later provided a safe house for Al-Qaeda leader Zawahiri.

The backbone of Qatar's policy has been to ensure that Saudi Arabia is not the only Sunni power in the region, and to this end, they have embarked on an aggressive foreign policy to further their ambitions. Their long-term approach is based on the belief that political Islam, which Saudi Arabia and other Sunni monarchies consider a threat, is in fact the future of the Middle East. They have been backing this horse for some time, and show no signs of stopping.

They have also hedged their bets by continuing to court the West. The Unites States has a huge base in Qatar and flies many of its aerial missions over Syria missions from the Al-Udeid air base. Qatar has joined the coalition supposedly leading the fight against ISIS—though it doesn't seem as if any of their air force sorties have actually bombed ISIS emplacements. At the same time, middle-men throughout the country continue to filter millions of dollars to ISIS affiliated organizations, which they claim to condemn. This has so far kept them in favor with both the West and the Salafi movement, who they consider the leading force of the future. But the United States has more recently been issuing increasingly stern warnings.

Salafism is effectively a hybrid of puritanical and political Islam; almost half of Qatari citizens are Salafist, and for decades the government of Qatar has funded think tanks, Islamic centers, and universities to preach this version of Islam. If they can be the sole backers of this future regional ideology, they will stand to become the epicenter of its power.

To understand Qatar's foreign policy, one need only look at their involvement in other conflicts, from Libya to Egypt. In Egypt, Qatar put its money behind the Muslim Brotherhood, giving Morsi five billion dollars as an aid package to shore up the economy and support the young, newly-elected government. This infuriated Saudi Arabia and other Gulf states who had always considered the Muslim Brotherhood and its form of political Islam a great threat to their rule.

But Qatar, believing this to be the future of politics in the region, took a gamble. Soon afterward, General Sisi overthrew Morsi with the help of the military, and received an aid package from the Gulf of twelve billion dollars. The Egyptian authorities promptly arrested three innocent journalists from Al Jazeerza; the Qatari-owned network. At the time of writing they are still being held in jail.

Libya

The first time Qatar played a major role in a war was in Libya, and they did so in an almost haphazard way. Qatar's policy was effectively to arm as many Sunni groups as possible to bring about the downfall of Qaddafi, and they did so by supplying them tens of millions of dollars, and twenty thousand tons of weapons!

So not only did Qatar take part in the US led bombing campaign, they also tried to fund as many different forces on the ground, hoping to create the biggest friendly network post conflict. The policy initially worked, but after the death of Qaddafi, the countless militias wanted to play a bigger role, and ended up at each other's throats, leading to the insurmountable problems we see there today. That being said, every side continues to show gratitude to Qatar.

Their policy in Syria has been much the same: identify as many Syrian ex-pats in Qatar as are willing, harness their connections to create networks on the ground, and throw money toward them. Initially, they were funding a myriad of groups, and almost anybody who approached them was able to raise vast sums by simply writing an itemized list of what they needed. Right up until early on in 2012, the United States simply let them get on with it believing that this would lead to the quick defeat of Assad, thinking this would be the quickest way to defeat Assad without having to get mired in the conflict—after all, nobody at the time anticipated the threat that would grow to be ISIS, and there is no evidence that Qatar ever directly funded ISIS, who are too extreme even for them.

But ISIS did develop as a direct result of the funding that flowed from Qatar to extremist groups, principally those that would eventually become the Jabhat al-Nusra and Ahrar al-sham. These were the most closely ideologically aligned groups in the region—both connected to Al-Qaeda and Qatar. Indeed, at the time of my writing, numerous Qatari clerics still offer vocal support to them via social media.

Another unforeseen result of all the funding from Qatar and other Gulf states was backlash from some of the groups they'd supported. Qatar gave money to as many people as possible and effectively let them fight it out for supremacy, imagining that they would gain favor with whoever came out on top. This led many fighters to believe that their jihad was being hijacked and corrupted by Gulf money—as a result, many moved to ISIS, which was seen as a more pure group.

Some of the fighters were quickly corrupted by the money and fund raisers also grew hugely rich. In some cases, they would simply multiply the amounts they needed many times over and keep the change, or, if handing over lists of fighters they needed to pay, add an extra few thousand names—the Qatari donors, in their need to be major players, simply did whatever was asked of them.

Kuwait

"Kuwait is the epicenter of fundraising for terrorist groups in Syria."
—David S. Cohen,
US Treasury undersecretary

Kuwait can be seen as the first nation to start really financing the Syrian opposition, and has been one of the major problems thanks to its long standing tradition of charitable donations and relaxed fundraising laws, as well as its sizable Salafi demographic. It was the perfect country from which to elicit funds. As opposed to other Gulf states, where charities have to be approved by the government, in Kuwait, they don't, and religious donations (which actually mean jihadi causes) are encouraged.

Even the ex-Kuwaiti minister for justice, Islamic affairs and Islamic endowments, Nayef al-Ajmi, has a history of promoting jihad, and has appeared on fundraising posters for Jabhat al-Nusra.

Kuwait has around one hundred thousand Syrian ex-pats (both Sunni and Shia), and religious fervor is high. So, from early on, adverts went out on social media, television, and radio, calling for aid to go to the fighters. This was seen as a perfectly reasonable demand, bearing in mind the fighters were Sunni and opposed the Shia and Allawite oppressors. High profile clerics went on TV calling for donations, and it is thought that hundreds of millions of dollars of private donations went to Syria via intermediaries.

This money was initially taken to Syria for aid, but toward the end of 2011, many donors believed that more was needed, and they began raising money toward fighting groups. As this escalation happened, the donors began playing a more politicized role and even interceding in how the war was fought—trying to set up mediation between warring groups to bring them together, or demanding specific targets.

As the war grew ever more violent, these contributions grew, and individual groups were getting hundreds of thousands of dollars a month each toward the cause. But this influx changed the battle on the ground.

Like that of other donor countries, fundraising in Kuwait followed a progression—as the conflict started, everybody was giving money, and people around the country gave even pieces of jewelry to raise funds, at the countless offices around Kuwait city. Some were told about set amounts to purchase specific goods for the fighters—eight hundred dollars would buy an RPG, for example, and initially everyone was trying to out-do each other, showing off how much could be raised. As time went on, however, and the groups began to fight amongst themselves, many of the donors saw their donations being wasted—after all, why should they give money so that two Sunni groups could fight each other?

Much of the grassroots donations began to dry up, and today those who still give money are the true believers, the very rich and influential—those who really want a say in the war. They use their money as a bargaining tool, trying to affect change in how the war is fought. They have other plans, too. It is not just the removal of Assad they're giving money toward, it's the creation of a Sunni state in Syria, and a new form of government—a whole regional redevelopment, which will next target Hezbollah and Iran. These people will never stop giving money—they see it as an investment in their religion.

CHAPTER THIRTEEN

Executions

"I refuse to call this hideous movement 'Islamic State' because it's not a state; it is a death cult."
—Australian Prime Minister Tony Abbott

In the ISIS capital of Raqqa, executions are simply routine—a part of daily life. A gathering place for locals, an activity for the fighters, and a constant warning to all. The swipe of a long sword, the sawing of a blunt knife, the excruciating agony of crucifixion, lasting days—all serve to terrify. The names and the crimes of the men are read out for the crowd: "Abdul Hassan, drinking alcohol, Ali Andome, insulting Allah; Feras Alrisy, stealing," and, as the men are brought forward, the surrounding crowd begins to cry out, "Allahu Akbar, Allahu Akbar"—God is great. The circle closes around the victims, often blindfolded, always resigned to their fate—heads hanging low.

Photo courtesy of Rick Findler

A rare picture of an ISIS prisoner held by Kurdish Peshmerga troops in Khanaqin, northern Iraq—June 2014.

Before an execution, residents are called to the town square—posters warn them of the upcoming schedule. Around one thousand can fit, and they bustle around the central circle, arching their necks to get a better view. The remains of bodies and heads lay around them, where the statue of Hafez al-Assad once stood. As the blood lust rises into a furor, people climb lamp posts, children are pushed to the front, and even women watch, all of them crying out.

The victims are brought from the prisons, where ISIS members fight over whose turn it is to kill next; they say it brings them closer to God. Among them, children as young as thirteen are sometimes given the honor. People are encouraged to watch and expected to watch, and if you miss too many executions, you might get a knock on your door: a stern lecture from a fighter, perhaps a few days in prison, perhaps a few lashes, you never know. So watching the executions has become commonplace—a way of life. Missing Friday prayers will certainly land you in jail, smoke, and you will be whipped, insult God, and you will surely die.

When the deed is done, the bodies are pulled to the side, the head kicked behind it, and the act repeated, again and again. Blood stains the pavements in market places, it seeps into the dust in roads and town squares, it permeates every part of life. Bodies remain strung up as a reminder to the rest—signs hung round their necks as a warning. And so people acquiesce.

The whole system is aimed at control—to impose Sharia laws and terrify the people—for although ISIS may have taken much territory, they must also hold on to it. This will be the test; conquest is one thing, governance another. With this in mind, they have done everything possible to instill fear in their people, and beheadings must surely work to that end.

CHAPTER FOURTEEN

Centralized Funding

The capture of Abu Hajjar in June of 2014 gave intelligence services their first insight into the immense wealth of ISIS. Hajjar, a courier for the head of the ISIS military council, Abdulrahman al-Bilawi, was caught at an Iraqi roadblock near Mosul. Following interrogation, he led Iraqi intelligence services to Bilawi's safe house. They found and killed Bilawi during a night raid, and discovered 160 flash drives of information. The information contained in them was a revelation, as they included names all foreign fighters and senior leaders, as well as details of their sources inside government, and a full breakdown of the group's finances.

It was the finances which really stood out, for until then, nobody had known the extent of ISIS financial gains. ISIS had achieved in just two years what other terrorist networks have been unable to do in decades: become financially independent. The ability to operate outside international banking systems is what has made them so hard to attack. They have not only earned vast sums of money (at the end of 2014 assets were calculated at anywhere between $1.3 and two billion dollars), but they have established a working economy, set up salary payments, and created a central financial system, which will be hard to break down, yet essential if they are to be defeated.

As an example of the wealth now floating around, one resident of Mosul said he had chosen to stay and profit, rather than flee. Having studied in Moscow (as many Syrians did), and being able to speak Russian, he became the principal supplier of satellite dishes and other goods to Chechens and Georgians fighting with ISIS. He claims to have made a fortune selling to these brigades, and in one deal alone sold ten plasma screens, five Internet satellite dishes, and fifteen high-definition cameras to a Chechen leader. The total bill was sixty thousand dollars, which the fighter counted out in cash.

Money is central to the ISIS story, and indeed, its ability to parlay wealth into early success on the battlefield is what made fighters flock to join. Numerous fighters and defectors have told me of the lure ISIS money holds—the ability to buy weapons and ammunition, pay salaries and bribes, maintain equipment, reward successful operations, and pay money to the families of those who have died all contribute to their strength. For many Syrian fighters, it is also a lifeline. In a country that has no functioning economy left to speak of, many fighters see ISIS as the only way to support their families.

Money will also be crucial to ISIS's future, for running a state as they do desire requires vast wealth. They must keep up the infrastructure of towns and villages, and hire people to do the administration. They also have to pay for their extensive media campaign. They are certainly aware of this, and early on set up finance ministers in both Iraq and Syria, and they are obsessive about keeping detailed records. In fact, their bureaucracy extends to all their governance.

What makes their financial independence so dangerous is the inability of the West to attack their income. Whereas with Al-Qaeda we could follow international transactions, and squeeze much of their wealth out of them (or at least pressure their wealthy donors with sanctions), with ISIS this is impossible to do. The bulk of money comes from within their own territory, and is now collected and transferred in cash.

They are able to generate tens of millions of dollars a month through the sale of oil, the ransoming of kidnap victims, and extortion, and they have stolen hundreds of millions of dollars in cash from banks and individuals. With this they are able to buy the loyalty of organizations around them—from Sunni tribes, to moderate rebels, to Lebanese militias.

ISIS claims to be against corruption, and indeed, unlike other groups, everything they earn goes into a central fund which is then paid out in salaries and expenses. They have a finance minister, and a strict code of financial conduct, which is instilled in their fighters upon initiation. Their constitution strictly prohibits any financial gain, saying:

"The wealth that was in the hands of the Safavid government (public funds) will be the responsibility of the Imam of the Muslims. He will dispose of it to the benefit of the Muslims, not to anyone who lays his hands on it, looting and plundering, or any action of the sort. If he does so, he exposes himself to legal action and accountability before the law followed by a deterrent punishment."

Prior to ISIS, leaders in other groups, from FSA battalions to local tribes, built up vast personal fortunes, and in turn many fighters left them or became greedy, trying to take over. However, ISIS is seen by its members and potential recruits as being untarnished by Gulf money, and as such true to the twisted values it holds.

Oil

In a small Turkish town on the border of Syria, which must remain anonymous, Adem is getting rich. Almost every day, he receives a new shipment of oil from across the border in Syria, and is able to turn it into great profit. Starting from early in the morning every few days, tankers, large and small, pull up on the Syrian side, full to the brim with diesel—refined and ready to go. A series of lookouts up and down the border keep watch, alerting him of any Turkish border guards, and then, depending on the shipment, he siphons either from one tanker to another, or straight into barrels. Within moments these are either loaded onto trucks and sent into the mass markets of Turkey, or held in a local house until the coast is clear. It's just that simple.

I asked him if he knew where the oil came from. "Syria," he replied, with a knowing smile. I asked about ISIS and if the oil might come from them, but he wouldn't be drawn. "It's the same as it's always been," he replied.

Initially, he used to lay pipes under the fields between the two countries. He'd use complicated pumps and motors to pump the oil into houses, and wait until dark. But now he says he doesn't worry so much, and he just changes location depending on the time of the shipment—wherever is safest at the time. Troops can't patrol the whole border, and so with his system of spotters, he moves up and down at will. "If the police are there, I pump here. If they come here I go there. They cannot stop me. If they catch me, I pay them."

The bulk of ISIS's money is made from selling oil this way, mainly into Turkey but also into Kurdistan. The total border length of roughly two thousand kilometers makes it practically impossible to stop, and the ISIS fields in Syria and Iraq continue to pump. They use long established black market routes, selling the oil at a fraction of true market value to dealers such as Adem who transport it into the main system. Once inside Turkey, it simply disappears into the system. According to Turkish media reports, smuggled diesel sells for $2.75 a gallon, while the official price in Turkey is more than seven dollars a gallon. ISIS is estimated to pump anywhere between thirty thousand and eighty thousand barrels per day.

In towns up and down the border, this game of cat and mouse goes on between Turkish villagers and soldiers. The Turks have long been known as traders, and as one saying goes, "If you have not been in smuggling, you won't find a bride."

Most amazingly, oil is also sold back to Assad, and in no small amount. Since ISIS first took oil fields in the east of Syria, there has been an agreement between ISIS and elements of the Syrian regime (or more likely middlemen) to keep the refineries pumping oil. I spoke to an ISIS defector who explained the mutual understanding. ISIS opens the pipes for a certain amount of hours per day and are paid millions in exchange—workers remain at the plants under ISIS control to make sure they continue to function, but the managers are changed to ISIS members with past experience in the sector. When asked how he felt about ISIS working with this sworn enemy, the defector replied, "It just is. If we cut off the flow the regime has said they will bomb the fields. Both sides need it."

In early June of 2013, oil income was estimated at one million dollars per day, however, some estimates put it as high as three million dollars. That Assad allows such money to flow to ISIS is at the heart of the theory that he has indirectly kept them strong to divert focus from his own murderous regime, as he hangs on to power.

The United States began to strike some of the refineries in October of 2014, as a means to cutting off this source of income, but it remains to be seen how effective this will be, and alone it certainly isn't enough. The United States plan to slow the sale of oil outside ISIS borders requires much work on the ground—identifying and tracking people like Adem. David Cohen, undersecretary for terrorism and financial intelligence, gave this warning:

"It is true, of course, that ISIS's oil moves in illicit networks that are largely outside the formal economy, where individuals are less vulnerable to financial pressure. But at some point, that oil is acquired by someone who operates in the legitimate economy and who makes use of the financial system. He has a bank account. His business may be financed, his trucks may be insured, his facilities may be licensed.

"The middle-men, traders, refiners, transport companies, and anyone else that handles ISIS's oil should know that we are hard at work identifying them. We not only can cut them off from the U.S. financial system and freeze their assets, but we can also make it very difficult for them to find a bank anywhere that will touch their money or process their transactions."

I'm not sure Adem will be worried.

It is clear that the organization includes business-minded people who invest its money. As the crisis of fuel escalates, stations selling gas have come under the ownership of ISIS. They reap a tidy profit from selling petrol back to the people they take it from—sometimes at four times the regular price.

Tightening their grip on the cities enabled members of the group to seize control of entrances and exits, not just for security reasons, but to impose tariffs as well. The tariffs vary in amount. The fighters get fifteen hundred dollars for every oil tank, two hundred dollars for large trucks, and one hundred dollars for medium-sized trucks that pass by.

Even if the West were able to stop the flow of the oil to Turkey, Assad, or southern Iraq, which they are certainly trying to do, ISIS has quickly developed an immense extortion racket, which for many years will keep them financed.

Extortion and Taxes

ISIS runs a sophisticated extortion racket, targeting

individuals, small businesses and companies to the tune of several million dollars a month. This started well before ISIS had even entered the Syrian war, and for a couple of years before their rise, ISI regularly threatened and attacked companies in Mosul, forcing them to pay to prevent attacks.

Once ISIS took Mosul, they continued their extortion. Ironically, now telecom companies are the only ones who no longer pay—telecoms being so important to ISIS that they actively protect the cell phone masts for them. Employees of these companies say business has never been so good, although other businesses have been ransacked, factories seized, equipment stolen and sold. ISIS fighters go door to door, business to business, from grocery shops to clothing stores, demanding cash; and those who don't pay receive a warning or a bomb.

Despite all this, there are many people in Raqqa who are happy that some semblance of life has returned, and they accept these payments as a tax. Raqqa's central bank is now the ISIS tax authority, where every two months shop owners come and pay twenty dollars for electricity, water, and security. They're happy as long as they see it as a better life than the chaos of war—it remains to be seen how long they can put up with the brutality though.

Banks still operate, though withdrawals are limited, and ISIS fighters have been known to stand outside and demand as much as ten percent of all withdrawals. Truck drivers are charged fees to use certain roads, the closer to Turkey the road, the more expensive the toll.

And in some cases, non-Muslims who have stayed— (there are very few) are allowed to pay a tax of $720 per adult male rather than leave. In theory, the Koran permits this, but in practice, ISIS kills or enslaves them. I have not heard of this actually being implemented, except in ISIS propaganda.

As far as their ability to keep up this governance, who knows. The official Iraqi budget for 2014 in provinces where ISIS operates was well over two billion dollars— much more than ISIS made. And so it remains to be seen how long they can keep up this financial burden, while also running an offensive military campaign over such a large area of land. Certainly, there have already been reports of water and electricity shortages—up to twenty hours each day in Raqqa.

There's no doubt that to reign in ISIS, its finances must be hit. If it can no longer pay its men, maintain and arm its weapons, and give the population food, water, and resources, then they will rise up, and ISIS will start to whither. At the moment, they still use Iraqi and Syrian banking systems, and this must be cut down. There are also rumors that they intend to mint their own gold, silver, and copper coins to create their now currency "The Islamic Dinar." The feasibility of this seems very low.

Kidnap

Kidnapping may not make as much money as oil, but it nevertheless offers huge profits. The majority of kidnappings are within Iraq and Syria themselves—ISIS take men, women, and children and hold them ransom before selling them as slaves or killing them. Christian families who fled Qaraqosh have told stories of having their babies taken from their arms, and being threatened with death unless they leave. Soon afterward, they receive phone calls demanding anywhere from five thousand to thirty thousand dollars for their safe return. A whole industry has been set up by middlemen who make these payments, and profit from the suffering of others.

Major money has been exchanged for the release of Western journalists whose countries are willing to pay for their release. ISIS demanded $132 million for the release of Jim Foley very shortly before his murder, though that figure is not in line with other payments made. Typical payments from Western countries are usually around five million dollars—negotiations begin at around twenty million dollars and then settled. Four French hostages were released in 2014 for eighteen million dollars.

The United Nations Security Council's Counter-Terrorism Committee estimates that ISIS took in forty-five million dollars in ransom in 2014, and the trend continues to rise. Al-Qaeda, more than ISIS, relies heavily on ransoms, and have earned well over one hundred million dollars around the globe over the last four years.

CHAPTER FIFTEEN

Khorason

As US planes began bombing targets in Syria, late on September 23, 2014, the world assumed they were attacking ISIS. But there was another group on their hit list that day, one that had previously hidden in the shadows, a small group known as Khorasan, or the Wolf Battalion.

That evening, Tomahawk missiles, fired from battle cruisers in the Mediterranean, rained out of the sky, striking a farm in Idlib province. The compound housed around fifty fighters of a bomb making group whose sole purpose was, and still is, to attack the West. That day, the missiles hit an explosives and munitions production facility, a communication building, and command and control facilities.

The attack shed light on the growing threat from within the lawless country, of groups that could plan and launch attacks on the West, with relative safety from the chaos, much as Al-Qaeda had done in Afghanistan. And indeed, the Khorasan group is a wing of Al-Qaeda, founded out of Jabhat al-Nusra, and their focus is on a repeat of 9/11. It's not destroying Assad or setting up a caliphate that drives them, but recruiting and training foreign fighters, and preparing them for attacks in the West.

The group was sent to Syria directly by the Al-Qaeda leader Al-Zawahiri and had been learning to develop external attacks, construct and test improvised explosive devices, and recruit Westerners to conduct operations. Al-Qaeda central leadership must give permission to allow its "franchises" to operate outside their regions, and it appears they've given their blessing to Jabhat al-Nusra to do this. As an example, Zawahiri allowed Al-Qaeda in the Arab peninsula (AQAP) to launch attacks elsewhere for Al-Qaeda. The main battle remains that against the West, whereas ISIS is (for the moment) still more concerned with the establishment of the Caliphate.

The leader of Khorasan and the main target of the attack in September was Muhsin al-Fadhli, a man well versed in attacking the Western world. According to reports Fadhli, "trains them on how to execute terror operations in Western countries, focusing mostly on means of public transportation such as trains and airplanes."

At just thirty-three, he had long been seen as a top commander amid Al-Qaeda, and is thought by some to have been one of the principal leaders of Al-Qaeda in Syria—the seven million dollar bounty on his head showing his importance to the group. He had been tracked by American intelligence for at least a decade, and it is thought that he died in the attack.

It is said that, as young nineteen-year-old, Fadhli

was one of the few who knew about the 9/11 bombings before they happened, and according to the United Nations, also fought against Russian forces in Chechnya, where he trained in the use of firearms, anti-aircraft guns, and explosives. He headed up an Iranian Al-Qaeda cell, and established a terrorist network in his native Kuwait, where he served jail time for helping to finance a terrorist organization. He is without doubt a global jihadist—moving from safe house to house, conflict to conflict.

He and the Khorasan group worked with Yemeni bomb-maker, Ibrahim al-Asiri, a member of Al-Qaeda in the Arab Peninsula (AQAP). It was al-Asri who is thought to be responsible for making the underwear bomb used by Umar Farouk Abdulmutallab in 2009 in his failed attempt to bring down a plane—it is this use of experimental explosives and delivery devices that is his trademark.

The repeated attempts to attack the West by this shadowy group have severely alarmed US officials. "The group's repeated efforts to conceal explosive devices to destroy aircraft demonstrate its continued pursuits of high-profile attacks against the West," said Nicholas Rasmussen, deputy director of the National Counter-terrorism Center. "Its increasing awareness of Western security procedures and its efforts to adapt to those procedures that we adopt."

And so, while ISIS is indeed the great threat in Syria and Iraq, for the land it's capturing and its potential threat to the region, the chaos around them has created a perfect breeding ground and safe haven for extremists from other groups, which must be dealt with, and in no half measure.

A Syrian child carries a gun, in the Northern city of Taftanaz—
May 2012

CHAPTER SIXTEEN

Children of the Caliphate

"ISIS prioritizes children as a vehicle for ensuring long-term loyalty, adherence to their ideology and a cadre of devoted fighters that will see violence as a way of life."
—United Nations Independent International Commission of Inquiry on Syria

Facing starvation and poverty, children living under the rule of ISIS stand no chance. They are lured into training camps from the age of thirteen, and groomed to become the next wave of fighters, suicide bombers, and killers. Some join willingly, but others are bribed with the promise of food, given up by their parents, or simply kidnapped. Stories from inside ISIS controlled areas tell of how they are manipulated and trained—it is well organized and planned.

All schools and universities have been closed under ISIS, so the only education is the one ISIS offers. Children under sixteen are first sent to boot camp. For forty-five days, they're brainwashed, indoctrinated into jihad, made to recite the Koran, and driven to fight. They're recruited to spy on the communities they live in, even on their parents, and they all swear allegiance to the Caliph, and promise to murder infidels. Online videos have shown these boot camps, where the children line up, chanting again and again, swearing allegiance to Baghdadi. There appears to be nothing half-hearted about their zeal, and as they place their hands into those of an emir and swear to ISIS, the smiles on their faces stretch from ear to ear.

Once the younger children have completed their religious brainwashing, they join the older fighters at military camp, along with the foreigners and the new recruits. Over the next three months, they receive lessons and are taught how to fire weapons, throw grenades, and make bombs. They watch videos of decapitations and mass murders, and are taught how grand these are. They're split into groups and given mentors—the suicide bombers, the bomb makers, and the fighters. One ISIS fighter who had been at a camp told me that many of the children plead to join the front lines or to be chosen for suicide missions. Before graduating, they are given dolls to practice their beheadings on. But sometimes they are made to decapitate a real human foe—the final dehumanizing act, from which there is no return.

Videos show scores of children in orderly lines, in identical black uniforms, being kicked, punched, and pushed around. As they fall or recoil, they immediately jump back to place, and shout their allegiance. They have sticks broken over them, and they practice patrols and maneuvers with real guns, which in some cases are half their height. They practice arresting and detaining prisoners, set up fake road blocks and ambushes, and again, each child in the videos seems to relish it (we must always remember it's propaganda).

Once training is over, they are brainwashed, deadly, and ready to die; they are sent straight to battle, or, if still under sixteen, recruited to carry ammo, cook, and wait for their own moment of glory. In the battle of Kobane, the dead bodies of young ISIS fighters were discovered at the front lines, clear evidence that ISIS sends them to the front, unprepared and untrained, whenever they need reinforcements. When there are many casualties, it is the young who are called upon for blood transfusions.

We can look at the examples of child soldiers in African countries who can be rehabilitated after fighting wars, but the difference there is that they are not being taught an ideology—they are simply drugged up and taught to fight. The children living under ISIS want to kill; they come to enjoy it, and they will hold it forever.

Here is one of the greatest problems we face. Inaction on the part of the United States does not only mean that ISIS holds territory, nor does it mean that they can somehow be contained. Every day that they continue to hold territory is another day that the children living under their rule are brainwashed against the West. This is the greatest threat, and one of the reasons this will define a generation.

In towns under ISIS control, it is these easily manipulated youngsters who often stand guard, their black armbands proudly on display. The blog "Raqqa is being Silently Slaughtered" tells a horrible story of how a son spoke out against his father, who had lied about his allegiance to ISIS. The father was beaten as the son looked on.

Even outside ISIS controlled areas, impressionable young children with access to the Internet are being brainwashed. I spoke to a Kurdish teenager whose Facebook profile showed the black flag of ISIS. He said that they were good Muslims, that they stood for good. He had no idea what they had really done, but to him it seemed fashionable. Some teenagers in Turkey wear black headbands and watch hours of ISIS videos, waiting for the day they too can go to fight.

But it is not only children in the region who are affected. Horrible stories have emerged online of children as young as four whose parents take them from England and France to Syria. Photos appear of them brandishing guns, and smiling under captions like "the next generation of Martyrs."

> *"Children as young as ten-, twelve-years old are being used in a variety of roles, as combatants, as messengers, spies, guards, manning checkpoints but also for domestic purposes like cooking, cleaning, sometimes providing medical care to the wounded."*
> —Laurent Chapuis, UNICEF Regional Child Protection Adviser for the Middle East and North Africa

CHAPTER SEVENTEEN

Abdul Rahman Peter Kassig

Abdul Rahman Kassig, twenty-six, was born Peter Kassig in Indianapolis, Indiana. He'd been delivering aid to people of Syria when he was kidnapped, and like the others, was held in horrific conditions before a video of his death was released on November 16, 2014. Despite his conversion to Islam, immense outcry from the Muslim world, and even an intervention by Jabhat al-Nusra on his behalf, nothing could save him. It just shows that they are intent on killing Americans, Muslim or not.

Kassig had been a US Army Ranger, and served a four month tour in Iraq. After being discharged, he moved to Lebanon and began working with refugees. He founded Special Emergency Response and Assistance, (SERA), a non-governmental organization to supply aid to the Syrians, and crossed over a few times. On October 1, 2013, he was kidnapped while en route to Deir ez-Zor, and found himself in a cell with John Cantlie and French journalist Nicolas Henin. It was here that he converted to Islam. Amid the torture, he smuggled a letter to his parents, which they released to the public:

"It is still really hard to believe all of this is really happening… as I am sure you know by now, things have been getting pretty intense. We have been held together, us foreigners … and now about half the people have gone home. … I hope that this all has a happy ending but it may very well be coming down to the wire here, and if in fact that is the case then I figured it was time to say a few things that need saying before I have to go.

The first thing I want to say is thank you. Both to you and mom for everything you have both done for me as parents; for everything you have taught me, shown me, and experienced with me. I cannot imagine the strength and commitment it has taken to raise a son like me but your love and patience are things I am so deeply grateful for.

Secondly, I want you to know about things here and what I've been through straight from me so you don't have to wonder, guess, or imagine (often this is worse than the reality). All in all I am alright. Physically I am pretty underweight but I'm not starved, & I have no physical injuries, I'm a tough kid and still young so that helps.

Mentally I am pretty sure this is the hardest thing a man

can go through, the stress and fear are incredible but I am coping as best I can. I am not alone. I have friends, we laugh, we play chess, we play trivia to stay sharp, and we share stories and dreams of home and loved ones. I can be hard to deal with, you know me. My mind is quick and my patience thinner than most. But all in all I am holding my own. I cried a lot in the first few months but a little less now. I worry a lot about you and mom and my friends.

They tell us you have abandoned us and/or don't care but of course we know you are doing everything you can and more. Don't worry Dad, if I do go down, I won't go thinking anything but what I know to be true. That you and mom love me more than the moon & the stars.

I am obviously pretty scared to die but the hardest part is not knowing, wondering, hoping, and wondering if I should even hope at all. I am very sad that all this has happened and for what all of you back home are going through. If I do die, I figure that at least you and I can seek refuge and comfort in knowing that I went out as a result of trying to alleviate suffering and helping those in need.

In terms of my faith, I pray everyday and I am not angry about my situation in that sense. I am in a dogmatically complicated situation here, but I am at peace with my belief.

I wish this paper would go on forever and never run out

and I could just keep talking to you. Just know I'm with you. Every stream, every lake, every field and river. In the woods and in the hills, in all the places you showed me. I love you."

© Photo by Sipa Press/REX

Peter Kassig, Aid worker, murdered by ISIS, November 16, 2014

Video

Peter Kassig's video is the only one I want to analyze in any depth, because it was different from the others, and his murder was not shown. It also provides an insight into how the media arm of ISIS works, and is symbolic from start to finish. The majority of the video shows the murder of a group of Syrian soldiers, each by a different foreign fighter—twenty-two of them in all. The image of Kassig's body only comes at the very end.

There are a number of carefully thought out symbols we can read into. The ISIS soldiers are wearing identical traditional military fatigues (adapted without a collar, giving them an Islamic edge), in a possible attempt to depict themselves as a legitimate Islamic army, rather than a gang of bloody terrorists (much of their propaganda seeks to show them as a well trained fighting force, which in many cases they are).

The Syrian soldiers they decapitate have been clean-shaven, though you can see the lighter skin where once there were beards. This could be an attempt to make them look less like Muslims—more like battlefield enemies rather than religious ones. Having come under increased criticism from the Muslim world, ISIS has become more careful about showing the murder of Sunni on Sunni, though it still happens daily. Instead, much of their recruitment seeks to address the Sunni-Shia schism.

Each of the twenty-two foreign fighters make a point of looking straight into the camera this time, without hiding behind masks, as they've done in so many other videos. It's as if they are challenging the viewer and the West to come and get them, and they say as much in the video.

Most significantly, it is filmed outside Dabiq, the town which, in the Koran, is the location of the great final battle between the crusaders and the armies of Islam. They make a point of addressing this and state that it's here they will draw the "blood of the infidels," and defeat any Western armies.

Many have wondered why the murder of Kassig itself isn't shown. I'd like to believe that he didn't allow himself to be used like this, and that perhaps he displayed the fortitude of a US Ranger to the end. The Ranger creed seems strangely fitting here:

"**R** ecognizing that I volunteered as a ranger, fully knowing the hazards of my chosen profession, I will always endeavor to uphold the prestige, honor, and high esprit de corps of my ranger regiment.

A cknowledging the fact that a ranger is a more elite soldier, who arrives at the cutting edge of battle by land, sea, or air, I accept the fact that as a ranger, my country expects me to move further, faster, and fight harder than any other soldier.

N ever shall I fail my comrades. I will always keep myself mentally alert, physically strong, and morally straight, and I will shoulder more than my share of the task, whatever it may be, one hundred percent and then some.

G allantly will I show the world that I am a specially selected and well trained soldier. My courtesy to superior officers, neatness of dress, and care of equipment shall set the example for others to follow.

E nergetically will I meet the enemies of my country. I shall defeat them on the field of battle for I am better trained and will fight with all my might. Surrender is not a ranger word. I will never leave a fallen comrade to fall into the hands of the enemy and under no circumstances will I ever embarrass my country.

R eadily will I display the intestinal fortitude required to fight on to the ranger objective and complete the mission, though I be the lone survivor."

Life goes on in the shells of demolished buildings. Aleppo, Syria.

CHAPTER EIGHTEEN

Christians Slaughtered

"The violent attacks that are sweeping across northern Iraq cannot but awaken the consciences of all men and women of goodwill to concrete acts of solidarity by protecting those affected or threatened by violence and assuring the necessary and urgent assistance for the many displaced people as well as their safe return to their cities and their homes. The tragic experiences of the Twentieth Century, and the most basic understanding of human dignity, compels the international community, particularly through the norms and mechanisms of international law, to do all that it can to stop and to prevent further systematic violence against ethnic and religious minorities."
—Pope Francis to Mr. Ban Ki-moon,
United Nations Secretary General

For the first time in nearly two thousand years, the oldest Christian settlement in the world has no Christians left. Where countless regimes and tyrants failed, the brutal terror of ISIS succeeded. Now many of the Christians who once lived in the Ninevah plains have fled north, bringing with them heartrending stories.

The few Christians that remain living under ISIS rule also face harsh, if not nonexistent, lives. They are not allowed to repair or build any house of worship (most churches have been taken over by ISIS as offices), they cannot display religious symbols anywhere, and they cannot disparage Islam.

I met some of these families in a church in the northern city of Sulemaniyah. In one corner lay a seventy-four-year-old lady, huddled under a piece of cardboard, trying to shield her face from the sun; her hip was broken, her voice almost gone, and she was wearing a diaper.

Unable to sit up, she recounted her family's escape from Mosul in a parched whisper. Having survived the endless ISIS shelling that demolished her neighborhood, she eventually left when they swarmed through the city. "We heard the gun shots outside our door, and knew the terrorists were killing Christians," she said. "But we hoped someone might rescue us. We cowered inside for two days, then knew we had to leave: we gathered some clothes and left at night."

"Street by street I had to crouch and sometimes crawl, until we reached the outskirts —I was sure we would be caught."

She made her way to the Christian town of Qaraqosh, but this too was soon overrun—now almost all the fifty thousand residents have fled. She then made her way to Erbil, but once there, was left on the streets with her family; six of them, between the ages of eight and seventy-eight.

They wandered the city for a few days, sleeping in gardens and on roads, before moving farther east. Here they found a church that could take them in, but every church here is full, trying to cope with the crisis.

"There were Christians everywhere we went. In every garden, and in every doorway, there are just so many with nothing and with nowhere to go. But I am so happy now we are safe, we are the lucky ones."

It's this sense of good fortune that is shared by many in the face of such loss, and the bravery of those who have nothing left is humbling. Many of the Christian refugees we have spoken to are merely grateful for the help they have been given, and happy to be alive; suffering in silence.

There is no doubt that this fortitude is the result of years of persecution. For many, this is not the first time they have had to flee. In fact, Christians here have been persecuted for decades, first under Saddam, then by a succession of jihadists groups.

Because of this, some of the Christian children today have never had a real home, always moving from place to place, always in limbo.

When I asked a ten-year-old called Aws, who had proudly drawn an orthodox cross on his arm, if he wanted to go home, he stared back at me… "No, this is nicer," he replied quietly, while surrounded by hundreds of refugees, sleeping thirteen to a room no bigger than one hundred square feet.

Aws's father was killed by jihadists when they first had to flee eight years earlier, and now he is fleeing again. As he told me, this time they left because "the bombs were too close, and the windows all smashed. Many people were dead."

His mother, who refused to give her name out of fear, told me she had spent the last few years saving to buy a home in her new village, but suddenly again had nothing. She cleaned the whole house before leaving it, hoping that perhaps one day she could go back.

In Christian neighborhoods, ISIS marks Christian houses with the letter N, standing for Nasare—a Muslim term for Christians, which derives from Nazareth. While they claim to offer Christians the right to convert, or pay a tax of $450 a month to remain, stories from other cities show this does not offer much protection. Across the border in Syria, ISIS is decapitating "Christian infidels."

When asked whether they had even considered converting, they emphatically replied no: "People say it would be easy to become a Muslim, but my religion is everything I now have—why would I give that up? I would die first."

Hundreds of thousands like her may still have their religion, but in northern Iraq, Christianity is dying.

One of the stated aims of the Kurdish Peshmerga, backed by US air strikes, is now to take back the Ninevah plains, and they pray that this will happen. "Please tell the world what is happening," they pleaded. "Please tell the world we just want to go home."

"Muslims are good people, our neighbors loved us," they insisted. "But we do not know who ISIS are and what they believe, we cannot imagine what they are thinking. We just want to live, we just want to be safe."

CHAPTER NINETEEN

Inner Working of ISIS

On Friday, November 7, 2014, fighter jets from the US led coalition attacked a gathering of ISIS leaders near Mosul. Witnesses claimed that the massive air strike targeted a house where ISIS officers were meeting, and at the same time, planes hit a convoy of ten heavily armed vehicles near Al Qaim, close to the Syrian border. For the next couple of days, rumors swirled that Baghdadi and other leaders might be among the dead. A nearby hospital was cleared of its patients, and cars fitted with loudspeakers circled the local town, asking for emergency blood donations—further emphasizing the significance of the injuries.

In online chatter that followed, though, it seems that Baghdadi had probably escaped (ISIS always announces its casualties soon after they've been killed). Iraqi sources claim that Baghdadi had been badly injured, but there is no evidence of this, and a few days later, he released an audio message stating he was alive. However, one of his principal aids and messengers, Abdul Rahman al-Athaee, was killed in the attack, as were fifty others.

Gatherings like this are incredibly rare for ISIS senior leadership, and it is still not known why they were meeting, or what sources the United States had inside. But the idea that cutting the head off ISIS through a targeted assassination might bring down the group is flawed. ISIS is set up in such a way that provisions are in place should this happen, and Baghdadi himself is not the only person capable of leading the caliphate.

In fact, Baghdadi is not even the highest force in the group, and although he does make all crucial decisions, and policy stems from him, he is technically below the Shura Council—the ISIS cabinet which chooses governors and members of the military council, and sees that Baghdadi's orders are adhered to.

Shura Council

Made up of between nine and eleven men, the Shura council has the power to make and overturn decisions, including those made by Baghdadi himself. It has existed since Abu Omar al-Baghdadi, previous head of ISIS, set up the rigid command structure that ISIS now follows. There have been rumors among defectors that Baghdadi is merely a figurehead—that the real decisions are made by others, perhaps those in the Shura council—but this is hard to verify.

Conventional research tells us that Baghdadi has handpicked the council himself, filling it with close allies who were imprisoned with him at camp Bucca, and who subsequently fought with him in Iraq after 2009, making it impossible that they would go against his word. Also on the council are the two men who are seen as his successors and could quickly fill the role of Caliph if required: Abu Muslim al-Turkmani, and Abu Ali al-Anbari.

Baghdadi has appointed Turkmani to oversee the twelve "regions" in Syria, and Abu Ali al-Anbari, the twelve "regions" in Iraq, for although ISIS strives for the single caliphate, they are pragmatic enough to realize that each country faces very different challenges, and until these can be aligned, they have separate governing structures in place for each.

Turkmani (real name Fadel Ahmed Abdullah al-Hiyali) was a lieutenant colonel in Saddam's military intelligence unit and close to both Saddam and Izzat al Douri, Saddam's brother-in-law who led the ISIS attack on Mosul. He was a special forces officer in the feared Republican Guard until Saddam fell from power. Like many other officers in the Ba'ath party, Turkmani then joined Sunni insurgents in their battle against the United States. Like Baghdadi, he was captured and placed in Camp Bucca, where the two overlapped for some time, and where they likely met. In his role as head of operations in Iraq, he oversees not only governors within the territory that ISIS has captured, but also a network of sleeper cells in territory that ISIS doesn't yet control, readying them to impose ISIS laws quickly should they conquer it. Turkmani is considered the principal heir to Baghdadi's reign.

Anbari, leader of ISIS in Syria, was a Major General in Saddam's army and also joined the Sunni insurgency in 2003. However, he was kicked out of Ansar al-Islam (another Sunni extremist group at the time) for corruption, before joining Al-Qaeda in Iraq (AQI), where he rose up the ranks to take charge of ISIS in Syria. It says a lot about the hypocrisy within ISIS that some of its own leaders clearly strive for power over beliefs, and merely use religion as a tool to harness their foot soldiers. Both he and Turkmani are in charge of overseeing governance projects and military campaigns—both have the brutal streak that comes from years in Saddam's military, and both have the discipline and military skills inherited from years of military training. Both would be prime candidates to take over in the event of Baghdadi's death.

Councils

Alongside the Shura council is the Sharia council, headed by Baghdadi himself. The Sharia council is in charge of doctrine and seeing that religious edicts are transformed into action. Very little is known about it, except it is made up of six powerful members, as was historically decreed in 634 AD by Omar bin al-Khattab, one of the most powerful and influential Caliphs of the past.

The military council is in charge of strategic planning, organizing raids, promoting officers, securing arms, and distributing bounty. It numbers between eight and thirteen members, and while Abu Ayman al-Iraqi is its leader, rumors suggest that the chief of staff may now be Omar al-Shishani, the Chechen fighter known as much for his military victories as his long red beard and hair.

The security council is headed by Abu Ali al-Anbari, Baghdadi's deputy in Syria and potential heir. It oversees the internal security of the organization, including the intelligence network tasked with routing out spies, Baghdadi's own security needs, infiltration of enemy forces, and the formation of suicide units. It is the security council that plays the key role in establishing the caliphate.

Governance

For a copy of the ISIS constitution, please see the appendix.

The security council, in charge of the feared internal security network, plays a crucial role in the establishment of the ISIS Caliphate, which is ironic, as they use the same brutal tactics as the regimes they seek to replace. In fact, many of the brutal practices are more alive and well under ISIS than ever before, and are run by the very people who ran them in the days of Saddam Hussein.

Activists within cities under ISIS control (such as the irrepressible bloggers "Raqqa is being silently slaughtered") report a constant state of fear on the streets, where even the slightest misdemeanor can result in jail and punishment. Working during prayers, smoking, and not attending beheadings, to name just a few, all invoke serious penalties.

ISIS is very aware that its grip over the population

relies on two things—a security service to stamp out sedition, and the ability to provide basic services. At the moment, the leadership is trying hard to impose a functioning civil society, but their reliance on fear as a method of control remains their most effective tool.

The big question for ISIS is whether they can give cities and territories a functioning level of governance fast enough, in which people see them as a long-term solution, and in which their brutality is at least tempered with positive governance.

In their attempts to do so, ISIS has quickly set about building up a network of ministries and government structures with which to complement its police and intelligence groups. They established religious, humanitarian, and judicial departments, and have been trying hard to show how their model for a caliphate will work. In some cases, such as in their strongholds of Deir ez-Zor and Raqqa, they have had relative success—at least compared with the chaos of battle.

They work in a pattern. Following the military conquest of a city or region, ISIS immediately sets up programs to enhance their humanitarian qualifications, opening bakeries, and supplying water and food, and oil and blankets during winter. Following months or in some cases years of war, communities welcome these initial acts of kindness, and reach the point where any form of governance, even at the loss of certain freedoms, is better than the chaos of war.

These are accompanied by outreach events, which are just like fairs, involving games and competitions with prizes; Koran reading competitions, Koran memorization, talks from leaders, interaction with fighters, and presentations explaining who and what ISIS offers are all on display in the town squares. They hand out leaflets, give out food and drink, and mingle with local people, showing their "friendly" side. They play tug-of-war, and host races and other games for the children. It's effectively their propaganda campaign to show how life under ISIS would be better than what they had.

Once they've consolidated their control on an area, and wooed people with their outreach programs, ISIS brings in their religious police. They impose harsh Sharia law and begin cracking down on anything that is contrary to their will, and by the time this has happened there is such a strong police state that revolt is unthinkable.

Though it has been said that there are people living under ISIS who are content. Ultimately, it's better for them now than it has been for the previous two years: the services are working (sometimes), they're getting some food, water and occasional electricity, and, other than the harsh rule, it's peaceful. The only attacks now in ISIS controlled territory come from the Assad regime, and these indiscriminate attacks mainly kill civilians, pushing some of them closer to ISIS. And so, when faced with the harsh reality of ISIS, where if you do what they say to the letter you're left alone, or the regime, which continues to attack and bomb the cities, some people pick ISIS.

ISIS has achieved this level of success by working closely with the systems that were previously in place under Assad: oil networks, water plants, road cleaning, etc. And while they'd ideally like to abolish all forms of the previous system, and cease working with "infidels," they've been pragmatic enough to strike a balance with the old, working with existing infrastructures, financial and otherwise, so that the cogs keep on turning. As a result, we see many of the same industries and banks continuing to work under ISIS control, continuing to move money around the country, and continuing to give some support to the people. It wouldn't be hard for the West to stop these from functioning, but that would lead to such a catastrophic shutdown that millions of people would starve or die.

ISIS's initial ability to supply electricity and water however, doesn't mean they can continue to do so indefinitely. Eventually, resources, parts, labor, will be needed from abroad, and with nobody willing to supply them, it will be harder and harder to keep the services up. In terms of workers and managers, they have had a large pool to choose from, however. Much of ISIS propaganda now calls for experienced managers and engineers to join ISIS from Saudi Arabia, Yemen, Tunisia, and other states. Again, this might work in the short-term, but if their plan is to rule indefinitely, they will need to begin teaching the next generation of students something other than religious education—something they seem unwilling and unable to do at the moment.

It seems likely that the United States will be targeting these cogs in the future to prevent ISIS from providing basic services. It is the assumption that in the long run, ISIS cannot continue to provide the services it currently does. As this happens, we will see people under ISIS turn against them, and ISIS resort to ever more brutal methods to keep people in check.

CHAPTER TWENTY

Sharia Life

Smoking is strictly forbidden under ISIS rule, and those caught can expect to be whipped, spend a few days in jail, or, if repeat offenders, killed at the whim of the "judge." Despite this, people have continued to find ways around the ban. In the capital city of Raqqa, a few stories have emerged that show both the resilience of the opposition, as well as the lengths some will go to in order to get their nicotine.

Having been caught on previous occasions, one resident of Raqqa has come up with an ingenious way to smuggle his tobacco home. It's still available for sale on the black market in the center of town despite the risks, and he goes twice a week to buy his share. People are regularly stopped by the religious police and searched in the streets so rather than walking back with his pack, for which he has been caught before, he ties it to the body of a homing pigeon, that he has taken to market to "sell." He releases the bird from the roof of the building where he buys, and by the time he gets home, it's waiting for him. Other people hide their cigarettes in packets of Acetaminophen, or inside stacks of bread.

Smoking is just one of the many things ISIS seeks to ban. They determine what is illegal through their extreme reading of Sharia law—the moral code under which ISIS expects Muslims (and indeed the whole world) to live. Sharia is central to their governance, and defines everything they do. It is a sign of their intent that they have opened more Sharia offices in their territory than any other kind. It is from these offices that edicts are made, and offenders prosecuted and punished.

The enforcers of Sharia are the feared religious police—The al-Hisba; it is they who are at the core of the ISIS police state, and central to the future rule of ISIS. It is ultimately the al-Hisba who enforce the strict rules determined by the Shura council, and more money is spent on them than on any other part of the "state."

Online propaganda pieces describe al-Hisba's aims as "Promoting virtue and preventing vice; drying up sources of evil, preventing the manifestation of disobedience, and urging Muslims toward well-being." They drive around the cities in specially marked cars, search people at will, stop them at roadblocks, check their phones and computers for contraband, and arrest them for displaying (or not displaying) appropriate images. Anything that represents Western values or hints at women dressing or behaving improperly is a serious offense. Western clothing such as jeans is forbidden, as indeed are any kind of tight clothing that shows the figure—male or female.

Courts

ISIS claims to have reduced crime throughout the territories it controls, and "judges" in the court system (appointed by the emir) have praised their own ability to reduce crimes such as looting and theft. At the same, time however, whole districts are being looted and robbed by ISIS fighters, who believe it is okay to steal from infidels, take their goods as a bounty of war, and rape, murder, and sell women. Numerous ISIS fighters Twitter accounts display the goods they've looted and the houses they've ransacked, and talk about the women they've taken—all with the courts' blessing.

These courts are everywhere throughout Raqqa, Aleppo, Mosul, and other central ISIS territories. Every day, judges hear complaints—from personal disputes about money or family, to theft, divorce, or crimes against religion. The crimes are heard, and the punishment netted out, but behind this facade, there are a huge number of detentions, arrests, hand chopping and other heinous acts that never reach the courts, which are subject to the whim of the enforcers. Prisons are full of people who are opposed to ISIS, have done nothing wrong, and who are subject to differing interpretations of Islamic law. It's a farce.

CHAPTER TWENTY-ONE

Foreign Fighters

Sitting cross-legged in a circle, the five foreign fighters appear on the screen in a peaceful oasis, amid lush plants and green palm trees. Speaking in almost dulcet tones, they don't display a hint of the war going on around them, save for the weapons they cradle gently in their laps. One by one, the men from Australia and the United Kingdom gently encourage others to join their fight. They talk about the glory of what they're doing, the peace in their hearts, and the happiness they feel; they beckon to the camera for others to follow, and playfully stroke each other's beards.

When an Australian man, Abu Yahya, speaks, a subtitle under his name announces his recent martyrdom (he died in battle shortly after the video was filmed); by the look of it he's already there—speaking peacefully of the heaven to which he refers.

Of course, this is just another cleverly choreographed and edited piece of film making, targeted at recruiting foreign fighters, but it's convincing. One only has to look at the sheer number of fighters flocking to join ISIS from the West to see how convincing it can be.

But the reality behind the foreign fighters is actually very different to this stylized scene. The truth is that the foreigners have an altogether different reputation within ISIS, and they're far from soft spoken. On the contrary, many of them are vicious; men who came to fire guns and cut off heads. For them, ISIS has little to do with Islam; it's just the means to get what they want.

I've spoken to ISIS defectors who were shocked by the brutality of the foreigners who joined them. They're full of blood lust; eager to kill, eager to inflict pain—many have a poor understanding of the Koran, and indeed quite a few are converts, or at least have "rediscovered" Islam recently.

The more appropriate videos for these men are the ones filmed by the foreign fighters themselves, not by the ISIS media machine. In one such video, a man with a thick South London accent and a balaclava addresses his "bruvas" back home: "While you're there on the block, watching that honey walk past, with your little batties (sic) on, and your hands down your trousers." He says, "Where are you when we start taking heads off, when we teach these guys a lesson," before firing off a gun. "Where are you when we gonna kill the Kufir."

And herein lies the truth behind many of the Western fighters—they come to be gangsters, to get street cred back home. I'm not saying that they don't believe in their "jihad"—indeed a number of Westerners have volunteered for suicide attacks (including an American from Florida, Moner Mohammad Abusalha)—but a large portion also want to go home eventually, as they realize that what they envisioned and what they got were two very different things.

They're just not trusted by the ISIS core. It's well reported that they're often made to stand guard, wash pans, carry bags, and cook food. They're the lowest on the chain—and when they do get sent to fight, it's to be canon fodder in places like Kobane. If there's a dire need for soldiers somewhere, they cut their training in half and send the foreigners.

This has resulted in a quite a few of them trying to go home. The French newspaper *Le Figaro* released a number of letters from French jihadists in which they sought a way back, claiming they had made a big mistake in coming. "I'm fed up," writes one. "They make me do the washing up. My iPod doesn't work any more here," says another. "I have to come back." A third is terrified about battle: "They want to send me to the front, but I don't know how to fight." The letters also indicate that a Frenchman who sought to follow his friend back to France was decapitated by his emir—a stark sign that, once you join them, there's no going back. In December of 2014, ISIS killed 120 other foreign fighters who were trying to leave.

This is what the campaign in the West needs to focus on—the ideological draw for "disaffected" youths back home—but little is being done to counter it. I suppose one view is that anyone foolish enough to be drawn to ISIS is better off there than in the West, and once they do go, they're flagged and placed on watch lists.

In the ISIS town of Manbij, north of Aleppo, for example, there are so many foreign fighters that it's been named "Little London" and "Little Berlin." So many have flocked there that up and down the streets Arabic is almost a second language. Some have brought their wives, some have brought their children—all of them are there for jihad. It's estimated by the US Department of Homeland Security that over twenty-seven hundred Westerners have gone from the West to fight with ISIS, including five hundred from the United Kingdom, seven hundred from France, four hundred from Germany, and over one hundred from the United States.

Joining ISIS is remarkably easy for foreign fighters. It's as simple as getting in touch with someone who's already there, buying a plane ticket to Istanbul, heading to the border, then crossing with your contact. The airports of Gazientep and Antakya, near the border, always have a steady stream of young fighting aged men, with few belongings, coming and going. There are even certain hotels which are known as safe for them to stay in.

Even for those further afield, in Australia, the United States, or Canada, there is no law against traveling around Europe, and you can buy Turkish visas at the airport. More and more extremists under prior surveillance are being prevented from leaving at the airport, and some have been charged with attempted terrorism based on texts and other evidence.

That being said, even if placed on a watch list at home, many slip through the net. In the case of Mohammad Ahmed Mohammad from Britain, he was already subject to a terrorism prevention and investigation measure (TPIM) in 2013, meaning he was out on bail, under constant surveillance, and was considered at risk of flight. One day, while being followed by undercover counter-terrorism police, he disappeared into his mosque, changed into a full length burqa, removed his ankle tag, and simply walked out the door. He has still not been found, and is thought to be fighting abroad.

Abu Hussein al-Britani (real name Junaid Hussain, twenty years old) is another man who has shown how dangerous Western fighters can be with ISIS. In 2012, he was sentenced to six months in a UK jail for computer hacking before joining ISIS in Syria, and he is now thought to be leading their advanced hacking program targeting journalists and news agencies.

Abu Hussein even had the audacity to reach out to demonstrators in Ferguson, Missouri following the riots there. "We hear you," he wrote online, "and we will help you if you accept Islam and reject corrupt man-made laws like democracy and pledge your allegiance to Caliph Abu Bakr and then we will shed our blood for you and send our soldiers that don't sleep, whose drink is blood, and their play is carnage."

Foreign fighters also post instructional videos for each other on how to get there and what to bring—warm clothes and other such things. There's a whole network set up for them—a network that needs to be closed. It's much easier for Europeans than Americans, due to the ease of crossing borders.

In the case of women, it's also easier. A sting was recently launched in the United Kingdom, where undercover reporters pretended to be teenage girls wanting to join ISIS. Shortly after declaring their intention to come, a contact from ISIS sent money to a transfer office in London for their tickets. A number of UK women have recently been stopped at the airports, but just as many have gone through.

Sixty-three women from France, fifty from Britain, and forty from Germany are known to have joined the ISIS ranks, offering to go and bear jihadist children. In September of 2014, a ring was broken up in central

France that specialized in recruiting girls to join for sexual jihad. The girls start online relationships with fighters before traveling to marry them. If their husband dies, they are lauded as the widows of martyrs, and free to marry again.

Some of them are so young, that it's hard to imagine they know what they're doing—what the religion or jihad even mean. Again, it's this stylized, idealized propaganda that persuades young, impressionable girls to join, including a number of sixteen year olds, a fourteen year old, and even a thirteen-year-old from Germany. Some have been known to travel with their young children, before posting images of them holding guns, or next to decapitated heads.

Jihadi John

The most famous foreign fighter is of course Jihadi John—the executioner. He is the man who has single-handedly murdered all the Western prisoners in the videos, and who has risen to become a symbol of the ISIS fight against the West. It is he who talks directly to the camera, directly to the Western audiences, while standing over his victims with a knife. He has now become a figurehead in his own right, and has risen to become a member of the Shura council. He is said to surround himself with British bodyguards, though speaks fluent classical Arabic—a rarity for Western fighters.

While US officials claim to know who he is, that

information has not been released. But there were initially many reports that he was Abdel Bary—a rapper and petty criminal from London. Aged around thirty, Abdel-Majed Abdel Bary was with ISIS before they joined the Syrian war, and was fighting with ISIS in Iraq. He boasted about his time in Syria on Twitter, showing a picture of himself holding a severed head in one hand, while the caption read, "Chillin with my homie, or what's left of him." Bary's father, Adel Abdul Bary, fifty-four years old, plead guilty in a US court in September 2014 to terrorism charges in relation to Al-Qaeda's bombing of US embassies in Kenya and Tanzania, and now faces twenty-five years in jail.

The big question is are these foreign fighters a threat to the West? Well, theoretically, yes. There is chance that they return home—be it to the United States, Canada, Australia, England or France—ever more radicalized than before, seeking to launch attacks there. But the truth is, Homeland Security flags practically every one of them who has gone—the time they spend abroad, where they spent it, and their profile. All offer serious clues as to where they've gone and what they've done. Realistically, there is a small chance of them making it back under the radar—and an even smaller chance that they are able to go undetected as they then plan an attack over time.

Foreigners at the Core

All this being said, there are two greater threats when

204 · INSIDE ISIS

we talk about foreign fighters. First, there are those who
are radicalized online, but choose to conduct lone wolf
operations at home, and don't travel abroad. These
people may not be on a watch list and are able to plan
attacks without being flagged. For example, the mur-
derers of Lee Rigby in London, who was butchered and
nearly decapitated in the street; the two Chechen brothers who blew up the Boston Marathon; the Australian
man who took hostages in a Sydney shop, killing two;
and the attacks in Canada that left two soldiers dead.
These were all direct results of the propaganda being
spewed by ISIS, and were carried out by radicals who'd
never traveled to fight. This is where the focus must
go—targeting people who proliferate or disseminate
radical propaganda.

The other great threat are the "real" foreign fighters:
those who make up the bulk of the army now devastating Syria and Iraq. These are the men from all countries
other than Syria and Iraq. They include Tunisians, Turks,
Kazakhs, Kuwaitis, Libyans, Algerians, Yemenis, Jordanians, Cambodians, Russians, Chinese, and Filipinos,
to name just a few. It's estimated that sixteen hundred
fighters from around eighty countries have flocked to
join. They continue to do so, and it's this mass migration that is the most serious concern. Many of them
have been through wars elsewhere, many are already
trained, and all of them are fervent believers in jihad.

They have no connection to the local people, and as
such are happier to commit atrocities against locals—in
this sense, they make the perfect foot soldiers. These are
the ones giving ISIS its might, and countries around the
world must be pressured to do more to prevent them
from coming.

These are the ones who could eventually return home to already fragile states, and expand the ISIS creed, destabilizing a whole region. Jordan, Saudi Arabia, Libya, Yemen—these are states which are close to the verge, and as much as we might think that it can't affect us in the West, it certainly can. The massive destabilization of the region could have serious ripple effects, and must be prevented.

CHAPTER TWENTY-TWO

Turkish Border

In April of 2012, as the Syrian conflict was in its infancy, we tried to cross the border. Late one night, we lay in a muddy ditch next to a barbed wire fence that separated Turkey and Syria. As we lay there holding our breath, just twenty feet away, Syrian Shabiha Militia scoured the area with torches; they were looking for us. It was one o'clock in the morning, and explosions lit up the horizon in the distance. For two hours we hid, huddled together in a tight ball, and listened as they talked. There was no doubt that had we been caught, they would have killed our fixers and taken us.

We learned that they had been tipped off to our location. There are countless pro-Assad Turks in the southeastern toe of Turkey that juts down along the Mediterranean, and as hard as we had tried not to be seen as we made our way to the border, the numerous car changes made it impossible.

After two long hours of dread, which we spent lying painfully still, they finally gave up and left. Not long afterward, two men carrying Kalashnikovs and wearing nothing but underwear came out of the brush ahead of us. Quietly they told us to undress and follow them. After a nod from our contact (a lieutenant in the FSA), we did as we were told. Moving forward through the brush, gripping our gear and our clothes, we must have looked ridiculous; a group of armed men in bright red underpants, followed by two semi-naked journalists sneaking through brush, toward the explosions in Syria.

Up ahead we saw a river, and the situation became clear. Wading straight in, we were quickly up to our necks, holding our body armor and bags high over our heads, as we strode through the cold water. On the other side we threw on our clothes and set off at pace through the olive groves and into the hills. We had entered Syria and were behind enemy lines.

The Syrian border is no longer controlled by Assad, and crossings like that soon became a highway for smugglers and fighters (they eventually built rafts in that particular place). Today, people queue up to cross back and forth both day and night, and you can see hundreds of refugees gathering at holes along the fence to flee, while other fighting aged men wait patiently to cross.

The border has become a lifeline for ISIS and other opposition groups, and it has put Turkey in the middle of a diplomatic storm. Their relaxed border controls have often led to accusations of support for ISIS, and while there's no direct evidence to prove this, at times it certainly looks that way. The reality is that Turkey is hedging its bets, trying to look decades ahead to its goal of usurping Saudi Arabia's power.

For Turkey, both Assad and the Kurds are bigger threats than ISIS, and because of this, and their rather neutral stance, they feel fairly sure that ISIS won't attack them. If they did, Turkey has 650,000 well trained soldiers to call upon—the second largest army in NATO after the United States. On the other hand, the Kurds, of whom there are anywhere from fourteen to eighteen million in Turkey, do pose a grave threat to Turkish sovereignty, as does Iranian influence in Syria.

Just a few years ago, Turkey was riding high in the region, and Foreign Minister Davutoglu famously declared in 2010 that, "not even a leaf can stir in the Middle East without us knowing about it." It is unsure therefore whether ISIS's rapid growth took them by surprise, or if in fact they saw it coming but recognized its potential long-term benefits: if played well, it could mean a friendly Sunni Syria to the south, the chance to secure gas deals with Iraqi Kurds, and the chance to limit Iranian influence around them.

Indeed, their ambitions know no bounds, and the Turks believe that with their new found political and economic power, they can become the region's main player. Along with Qatar, Turkey backed the Muslim Brotherhood, placing their faith in that kind of political Islam becoming a major force of the future. President Erdogan himself has moved closer and closer toward an Islamic state.

So when the Syrian conflict began, Turkey was one of the first countries to openly support the uprising against Assad. Assad's fall would leave a vacuum that would allow Turkey to spread its influence south and help achieve Erdogan's goals. In early 2012, his Foreign Minister Davutoglu laid these out in parliament, saying, "We will lead the wave of change in the Middle East; a new Middle East is being born. We will continue to be

the owner, pioneer, and servant of this Middle East."
Could Turkish acceptance of ISIS be part of this strategy;
could they be waiting while others countries get mired
in the problem?

Turkey and ISIS

The one condition Turkey has constantly demanded in
exchange for their help is an agreement from the United
States that Assad be removed. As the United States are
now unwilling to offer this (for fear the vacuum would
be filled by ISIS), there remains a stalemate between
the two. Until there is a group able to fill the gap that
would be left if ISIS was defeated (other than Assad or
the Kurds), Turkey will sit on the sidelines.

Early on in the conflict, the United States was happy
for weapons, money, and fighters to flow across the
Turkish border to more moderate groups in the fight
against Assad, and Turkey was (and is) happy to do this.
Obama believed that regional powers could influence
the war, bringing it to a quick conclusion, and that he
could stay out of it, but as Assad held on and sectarian
crimes grew more heinous, ISIS thrived. Despite the
rise of ISIS, Turkey has done little to control the flow
of ISIS oil or fighters across the border, and little to
change their policy.

When I mentioned to an ISIS defector that Turkey
might crack down on the porous border, he simply
laughed. "The border is no problem for us," he
responded, "nor is Turkey." He added that they simply

changed clothes or claimed to be FSA while crossing, and were never stopped.

Turkish Security Services (MIT) do closely monitor ISIS activities, as one amazingly detailed report on their movements, published by the Turkish Governor of Hatay, a province along the border, shows.

"ISIS operatives began to assemble in the town of Darkush in March, going by bus to the Zurzur area on March 14, 2014. Three hundred meters from the village of Kolcular at the closest point to the Turkish border a group of around 150 stayed the night in a two-story villa. On March 15, 2014, they crossed into Turkey in groups of forty-five to fifty at four separate points. They were met here by a person by the name of Abu Bara and taken to the Kent Hotel in Reyhanlı at around 6 a.m. on the same day."

Despite intel like this, fighters are rarely arrested, and there are rumors that ISIS fighters cross over from Syria and Iraq just to dine on kebab in southern Turkish restaurants. It is also known that wounded ISIS fighters are treated at private Turkish hospitals near Antakya, and allowed to recuperate.

The signals coming from Turkey therefore clearly show them playing both sides. At various times, they have negotiated with ISIS (such as for the return of forty-five diplomats seized in Mosul—a deal that is rumored to have included the release of ISIS prisoners); at other times, they have fought against ISIS (a few cross border skirmishes). They have worked with the Kurds, and then cut them off when they were most needed. They openly claim to support the United States, yet have given no permission for their country to be used to launch airplanes. They do little to stop ISIS oil from being sold across the border, and knowingly allow ISIS fighters to operate in Turkey, but claim to forbid both. So just what is their aim?

Leaks

On March 27, 2014, a secret recording was leaked of a meeting between high-level Turkish officials. The recording, released on YouTube, laid bare much of Turkey's policy toward ISIS and Syria—it also led to a countrywide ban on YouTube.

Most damning of all, Hakan Fidan, Turkey's powerful spy chief and head of the National Intelligence Organization (MIT), can be heard proposing to stage a fake ISIS attack on Turkey, suggesting it could be used as a ruse to justify operations in Syria.

"I'll send four men from Syria if that's what it takes," Fidan can be heard saying. "I'll make up a cause of war by ordering a missile attack on Turkey.... Second after it happens, it'll cause a great internal commotion."

The country recoiled at Fidan's idea, and it led to a huge domestic scandal, but most significantly, it shed light on one of Turkey's possible long-term goals—the recapture of the southern Aleppo province. Historically, Aleppo is Turkish, but after the fall of the Ottoman Empire, and the end of the First World War, it was taken away. The reason Fidan suggested an incursion into Syria seems not to be to take on ISIS, but rather to gain control of the Tomb of Suleyman Shah—a Turkish shrine inside Aleppo, which is already Turkish sovereign territory. It's not inconceivable that in the chaos that ensues over the next few decades, Turkey will make a claim over the area.

The tape also shed light on how uncertain the Turkish government was. Throughout the nine minute clip, other attendees, such as Foreign Minister, Ahmet Davutoglu, and Deputy Chief of the Armed Forces General Staff Yasar Guler, debate a variety of options.

Davutoglu laments not being decisive sooner and complains that, "national security has been politicized. All the talks we've done on defending our lands, our border security, our sovereign lands in there, they've all become common, cheap domestic policy tools."

And herein lies Turkey's problem. They seem to have been stifled by their own domestic upheavals, and their inaction has led to the accusations of supporting ISIS. Whereas they once had the opportunity to influence events, they never gave support to the right people when they had the chance. As Foreign Minister Davutoglu says in the recording, "If only we'd taken serious action … in the summer of 2012."

Return to Turkey

When Rick and I crossed back from Syria to Turkey following a few days in Idlib, we had a very different crossing than when we'd entered. Assad's troop movements had forced us to cross about sixty miles north of where we'd entered, and although we would no longer be up to our necks in water, the crossing would be just as fraught.

Having had a very rough few days avoiding Assad's

troops, witnessing the results of terrible brutality, and with little to eat and very little sleep, we were pleased to be returning. As we made our final approach to the border over the hills on foot, we looked down to see a long stretch of barbed wire without much cover. It wasn't ideal at all, but we were tired and afraid and we wanted out of Syria.

We were with our Syrian fixer and an FSA fighter who needed supplies from Turkey. Our crossing would again be illegal and if caught, we'd be in big trouble. Both of them suggested we sleep in a nearby shepherd's hut until morning, so we could reevaluate our crossing in daylight and get a better look, but with the last few days behind us, I made a judgment call—a bad one. "I'm going," I hissed at the fixer. "You guys can wait, but I don't need anyone's help to walk that far," and off Rick and I set.

I knew that he wouldn't leave us behind—his job wasn't complete until we were safe and back in Turkey—so he came with us. Like many of the Syrians we've worked with, he was a kind, honest, and gentle man—caught up in this tragedy. He and the FSA fighter followed us reluctantly.

We stumbled down the rocky hills, trying to hide behind any bushes we could find, jumping down rock faces and scraping ourselves on the brambles and thorns but forging on. It was tough work, and when we finally made the fence, numerous rolls of barbed wire faced us—many more than we'd expected. We couldn't find a place to cross, and crawled up and down the border until finally we pushed some of the fence down, and began scrambling into Turkey.

Each of us was getting caught in the barbed wire, and

the more we tried to free ourselves, the more caught up we became—our clothes catching and tearing. It was a horrible feeling—unable to move forward, unable to go back—but eventually three of us got through. As we turned to help the last man—the fighter, who was still caught up—a giant flash of light lit us all up and shouts erupted. Running toward us were armed men—their guns trained on us.

Rick and I fled immediately at full pelt. We were still in full body armor which is heavy at the best of times, but you don't feel it when you're fleeing. As we sprinted inland toward some trees, the men opened fire—shotguns. We heard the pellets rushing past us and around us, and we split up. I threw myself over a stone wall and kept running toward a small farm, while Rick threw himself down a steep drop. We were on the outskirts of a village and I could still hear them coming and shouting so I headed toward the farm. From nowhere, Rick leapt in front of me still running—he'd seen the same building.

We threw ourselves over another wall and under an outdoor staircase surrounded by hay. Our hearts were pounding, and we tried to make as small a shape as possible, crouching, huddling together in a tiny ball. For twenty minutes they searched, walking up and down no more than ten meters away, but they didn't find us. I actually remember being afraid of the beads of sweat that were falling, thinking they'd give us away, and trying to catch them before they hit the ground.

After it went quiet, we headed into the farm, and jumped over another wall, which immediately gave way beneath us. We tumbled down the other side in a pile of rocks and, looking up, came face-to-face with an angry

Turkish farmer. Still in our body armor, in the dead of night, two Westerners would have looked suspicious to say the least. The farmer shouted and made a grab for us, but Rick threw him away and we set off again.

To cut a long story short, we soon turned on our Turkish SIM cards to discover that our fixer and the fighter had been arrested by Turkish border police. They accused them of being terrorists, not believing they were with journalists. In the end, we actually had to walk back to the border with our hands up and turn ourselves in.

The two Syrians were sent back into Syria (only to cross to Turkey again a few hours later) while Rick and I spent the next day and a half in a Turkish cell—the same cell that the amazing *New York Times* reporter Anthony Shadid was held in just months before his death as he left Syria. His name was before ours in the entry log.

A couple of days later, we were interrogated by the Turkish intelligence (MIT) and deported from Turkey.

CHAPTER TWENTY-THREE

Syria's Kurds and Kobane

On September 24, 2014, I received a desperate call from a Kurdish intelligence officer. The town of Kobane on the Turkish-Syrian border was under siege. ISIS was only a few miles away, and tens of thousands of refugees were still there, at risk of being slaughtered. The Turks had been preventing many refugees from escaping to Turkey, and were also stopping reinforcements from going in to help. If nothing was done, it would be a bloodbath.

Soon afterward, the media began covering the town extensively (a number of other journalists received the same call), and in the face of a possible massacre, the United States was forced to act. Kobane quickly became the first symbol of US action against ISIS, as hundreds of journalists from the world's media gathered on the safety of a hill in Turkey, while a ragged group of fighters held on inside the town. United States planes and drones circled overhead for weeks, a constant sight in the sky; they bombed ISIS emplacements, and they even bombed the hill where ISIS had placed a flag—hardly a valid target in the grand scheme of things, but a great media stunt.

A Kurdish fighter looks out at ISIS emplacements at frontline near Kirkuk, June 2014

On the surface, it appeared that the United States was taking the fight to ISIS, as Obama had said he would. However, for all the talk of US intervention, the truth is that Kobane was more of a smoke screen than a genuine target, and that it was used more for publicity than as a real strike at ISIS. In every interview for the next six months, Obama held up the action in Kobane as evidence that he was doing something—as if he was looking for short-term success rather than a long-term strategy against ISIS. It was "The CNN Factor."

I certainly don't want to suggest that the US action

was worthless—it wasn't, and there's not a doubt that their response helped save many lives. But Kobane is of no great strategic importance to ISIS, nor was it even close to the most significant battle being fought. ISIS already controlled large parts of the Turkish border—this would give them just a few hundred meters more.

What ISIS did achieve by forcing the United States to defend the Kurds in Kobane was to remind Turkey that the Kurdish threat was very much alive and well. The Kurds in Syria (YPG) had been given effective autonomy by Assad early in the conflict in return for not fighting against him, so ever since the outbreak of the conflict, Turkey has been terrified that they might create another Kurdish state on their border as they have in Iraq.

As a sign of Turkey's indifference toward ISIS, video footage emerged of armed ISIS fighters approaching the Turkish border and talking calmly to Turkish border guards before waving good-bye, being picked up by an ISIS pickup truck, and returning to Kobane.

It's also possible that ISIS sent under-prepared, under-trained fighters to Kobane in an attempt to divert US air strikes away from other more important battles—while the world's focus was on Kobane, ISIS was conquering territory throughout Anbar province in western Iraq, unimpeded.

ISIS also needed the victory for their own propaganda, and to keep up the image of "baqiya wa tatamaddad," their policy of "remaining and expanding." They fought alongside a number of Islamic front groups, and in this sense it was a great example of collaboration between various opposition groups against ISIS. Once they started the battle, they sent hundreds of untrained young troops to fight there and die. This included two British men who were killed fighting for ISIS, while across the lines two other British men had joined the fight for the Kurds. It was the first known case of foreigners fighting one another on different sides of the war.

The Turks effectively see the US support for the Syrian Kurds as completely anathema to their own goals, and if anything would rather have an understanding with ISIS. Even though Abdullah Ocalan, the founder of the Kurdistan Workers Party (PKK), considered a terrorist group by many Western countries, wrote a letter from prison in March 2013 claiming their thirty year war with Turkey (costing the lives of thirty thousand) had ended, Turkey nevertheless began bombing PKK emplacements in October 2014—a clear sign that group at least remained terrorists.

The fact that the United States is supplying weapons to the Kurds in Iraq, and that Iraqi Kurds have traveled to fight in Kobane, makes it appear to Turkey that the United States is arming the PKK—and again, Turkey must look ahead to the disorder that will remain when other parties have left, and does not want those weapons to be used against it.

CHAPTER TWENTY-FOUR

Iraqi Kurds

Rockets and mortars peppered the vast plain below us as Kurdish generals surveyed the battlefield. Plumes of smoke rose around the landscape as rockets streamed over our heads, and the sound of gunfire erupted endlessly. As a tank roared backward, ambulances headed forward into the dust.

Rick Findler and I were embedded with Kurdish Peshmerga fighters, near the northeastern town of Jalawla, where troops were battling to hold back ISIS forces. Five days earlier, ISIS had swept into Mosul and across the country, trying to push all the way to Baghdad, but the Kurds stood in their way. It was one hundred degrees, and on the other side of the dusty plain, about two kilometers away, was the enemy. We could see their newly captured Humvees moving along the ridge, and their black flags flying.

The vast open space between us was like a medieval battlefield; shells and rockets flew back and forth, striking targets on both hillsides. Heavy caliber machine guns spat their bullets across the plains and peppered the landscape. Rockets and mortars were targeted by people with pencils and paper, as they tried to calibrate the tubes.

Without warning, rockets screamed repeatedly over our heads from just behind us, passing dangerously close. Huge cheers erupted as they hit the other side, but neither side seemed to be striking decisive hits. ISIS had far more advanced weaponry than the Kurds, and the Kurds could do little but defend themselves, striking with the occasional rocket, then moving quickly to launch somewhere else along the ridge.

Suddenly a helicopter appeared above us—it was the Iraqi Air Force. There was another cheer from the Kurds as it circled, for it was rare to see cooperation between the two sides. As the helicopter hovered above, a missile suddenly launched from under its belly, snaking straight toward us—a split second later, a car full of Kurdish soldiers a hundred meters away exploded in flames. We stood confused, dumbfounded, looking around. Panic broke out. In a mad scene of chaos, hundreds of soldiers began sprinting in every direction; Rick and I dove in a ditch and hugged the bottom, our faces in the dust, piled up among with soldiers—but the damage was done. As we leapt in another car, we passed the wreckage. Amid the flaming wreck nothing was alive.

Eight Kurdish soldiers had died from two "friendly" rocket strikes, and as we fled, the fury and disbelief was palpable. The Kurds were convinced that the Iraqis had done it on purpose, and such is the animosity between them that this view is still widely held.

That day is a perfect analogy for Kurdish strife, and how they see themselves. Underarmed, undersupported, fighting on all fronts with antiquated weapons and regularly stabbed in the back by allies. In the past, they have had to battle Saddam, Turkey, Iran, the central Iraqi government, and now ISIS, yet they are the only true Western ally in the region.

Kurds are the largest ethnic group in the world without a state. Their territory, straddling land in Iraq, Iran, Turkey, and Syria, has been brutalized throughout history. They have been slaughtered en masse, and persecuted. They are rare in the Middle East, as a people whose identity as Kurds comes before their religion (the vast majority are Sunni, but some are Yazidi, some Christian, even a few Jewish), and in northern Iraq, they have founded a democratic, Westernized, friendly state.

It took everyone by surprise when ISIS decided to attack the Kurds in Mosul Dam and Erbil. Everyone believed that after ISIS had swept into Iraq, they would continue their push south to the holy cities of Karbabla and Najaf, then onto the great prize, Baghdad. But for no apparent reason, they moved north. It may have been because the Iraqi Kurds had been helping the Syrian Kurds in their fight against ISIS; it may have been because ISIS knew that sooner or later, they would be drawn into the battle by Western allies, or it may have been quite the opposite—attacking the Kurds to entice the United States to fight.

For once, the United States responded, to protect the Kurdish capital of Erbil and the Western workers and oil offices based there. Once the first US bomb had been dropped on Arab lands, once the United States had no option but to intervene, ISIS could paint the picture of a new crusade led by the United States. It certainly hasn't hurt their recruitment drive, and they always seem delighted to fight the "infidels."

© Photo courtesy of Rick Findler

Kurdish troops fire rockets at ISIS emplacements near the town of Jalawla—June 2014.

Independence

Prior to attacking the Kurds, ISIS had actually helped them out in many ways, and from the Kurdish point of view, the ISIS blitzkrieg into Iraq had some benefits. As the Iraqi army disintegrated, fleeing their posts, the Kurds moved swiftly to take control of the long disputed, oil rich territories to the south which ever since the days of Saddam had been disputed with the central government. Saddam had gone as far as undertaking a process of Arabization in order to change the demographics: slaughtering, gassing, and terrorizing the Kurds while moving in Arab families. So for the first time in decades, when ISIS came and the Iraqis fled, the Kurds controlled their traditional lands again.

In fact, almost every Kurdish soldier I spoke to in the early days of the war saw ISIS as a means to gaining Kurdish independence, and there were even rumors of an agreement between the two sides. ISIS would push south, and the Kurds would not attack from the north, holding the borders of their newly claimed territory. But when ISIS finally did attack, and the Kurds were forced to defend themselves, they found themselves seriously under-prepared.

For decades the Kurds fought in the mountains as an insurgent forces—they were the small groups that confounded the huge standing army of Saddam. But with ISIS, they found the roles reversed—they were suddenly the national force taking on insurgents in the open plains, no longer secure in their mountain hide-outs. Nor had they been allowed to update their army or acquire modern weapons, which the government in Baghdad has to approve. So they were struggling to hold on.

The border between Kurdistan and Iraq is thirteen hundred kilometers long, and this suited ISIS tactics perfectly. ISIS forces moving quickly in pickup trucks were able to probe the lines in various places, and the Kurds were simply unable to keep up. Much has been written of the brave Kurdish Peshmerga, who had held back ISIS troops, but the reality was very different, and the Kurds were only just able to hold them off.

Although the Kurdish fighters of old are known as fierce warriors, the young Peshmerga lack these same skills. Not only has there been relative peace over the last twenty years, but the Kurdish armed forces are hampered by a system that is riddled with corruption and nepotism. On many of the front lines that I have been to, inexperienced troops were being taught basic military skills having just arrived that day, and trying to catch up and learn to fight.

"We need the United States for everything now," a member of the Kurdish special forces said to me. "We must be taught how to establish units, how to get a better chain of command, how to fight and how to be unified."

CHAPTER TWENTY-FIVE

Kurdish Arms Bazaar

Business is booming for the gun sellers of northern Iraq. From over-the-counter sales of American M16s, to back-alley dealings for RPGs there is a market for everything, and with it come daily fluctuations in price.

In September 2014, I visited an illegal arms bazaar in the Kurdish district of the City of Kirkuk, where people flock to buy, sell, and trade weapons of all types and sizes. Similar markets have popped up in most towns around the region.

Lining the streets, dozens of vendors displayed their goods as customers perused the items. On upturned boxes lined against walls, piled on tables, and hanging from pegs; weapons were everywhere, being placed in boxes and bags, and on carts. AKs, M16s, M4s, RPGs, grenades, crowd control guns, pistols, and heavy caliber weapons were all available en masse.

A month earlier, there had been a suicide bombing after an Arab man walked into the area detonating his device. Two soldiers and three civilians were killed in the attack, but the market continues to operate, shifting its location when needed.

Although technically illegal, as gun buyers require a license, many of the customers are military themselves. Kurdish army troops have to buy their own weapons, and those who can't afford to buy them on the regular market can find discounts here.

One vendor told us he would give fifty percent off to Peshmerga soldiers who were fighting "the Arabs," and indeed Arabs (of whom there are many in this divided city) are not allowed at the market. Another told me, "I wouldn't sell a gun to an Arab if you gave me one million dollars." Entry level AK-47s for those with little money are often marked with the year they were made, and many we saw were pre-1980.

However, it is still the weapon of choice in the region—mainly because its ammunition is more common, it is amazingly reliable, and it's far cheaper than the US models. But the prices fluctuate daily based on the proximity and significance of battles, and the rise and fall of panic.

Two years ago, the cost of an AK-47 was a mere three hundred dollars, but with the Syrian conflict intensifying, prices rose to an all-time high of fifteen hundred dollars. Now they stand at seven hundred dollars. There was a recent surge in prices following the ISIS take over of Makhmur, but then a decline following US bombing.

Prices also dropped following the flight of the Iraqi army, as the region was suddenly awash with weapons. Canny dealers along with civilians got hold of stockpiles, either selling them to other dealers, or becoming dealers themselves.

Many of these guns were US M4s and M16s, which

are a real status symbol among the troops. While the M16 is generally considered a better gun, it sells for less than the M4 due to its larger size (it's a vanity thing). The M16 sells for three thousand dollars and the M4 for six thousand dollars. Handguns range from twelve hundred to twenty-five hundred dollars, RPGs cost two hundred dollars with one rocket, and a BKC machine gun five thousand dollars.

The price of Kalashnikov bullets has now overtaken that of other rounds due to demand, with one Russian 7.62mm round costing seventy-five cents, and one US 5.56mm round, fifty cents.

An enterprising young boy had set up a hunting knife stall, and as people stocked up on a variety of weapons, he did brisk business. After a purchase, they left, their guns wrapped in black garbage bags.

© Photo courtesy of Rick Findler

A Kurdish soldier looks out over Diyala province, Iraq

—June 2014

Peshmerga—Those Who Face Death

Aging Peshmerga fighters, many in their fifties and sixties, are rejoining the Kurdish army to fight against the Islamic State in Iraq. Faced with an ever growing threat from the well armed and battle-hardened extremists, Kurdish men of all ages have been flocking to protect their borders.

Spurned on by their families, they have gathered from around the world, brought back by a sense of duty, and of shoring up an army in desperate need of support. From England, Sweden, Syria, and elsewhere, the Kurdish diaspora have returned to fight. Solicitors, taxi drivers, restaurant owners, and retirees now carry guns alongside the younger recruits.

For decades, the Kurds have fought their foes from the mountains, but many of the new recruits are untrained or have little experience. As such, they are turning to some of the old and much admired fighters of the past to boost morale among the young.

At the front line in Tuz Khormato, a group of old soldiers gathered under the leadership of their old commander, General Abdullah Musla, to fight once more. Over the past twenty years, they had spread far and wide, but this week, they sat together again, to face another threat.

An almost mythical figure in modern Kurdistan, General Abdullah, known as the "Dark Lion," commands huge respect. He was among one of the first Peshmerga, enlisting in 1967, and has fought against a multitude of enemies. Wounded fourteen times, he has scars covering his sixty-four-year-old body, and has lived and fought in the mountains for years. Still energetic, he insists "I have never tired of being a Peshmerga"—a word which means literally, those who face death.

In June 2014, he began to receive calls from his old soldiers asking that they be allowed to fight again. Today he has at least a dozen of them by his side, and the same is true in battalions around the region.

In mosques everywhere, queues to enlist stretch far—as a mix of young and old try desperately to join this battle. Such is the demand that people are now being turned down by the army, and those who are accepted into the force are made to buy their own guns.

When questioned about the physical health of the older, returning fighters, the chairman of Retired Peshmerga Soldiers, Abdul Kanibardi, sixty-four years old (himself newly enlisted), replied, "One never forgets how to use a gun." Others added that they would fight until the end, and were not afraid of death; they often lead the defense when ISIS attacked their lines.

Many might think that allowing aging soldiers back into the army based solely on service they did twenty years earlier, without making them train, might be misguided, especially when turning down able-bodied men.

But for better or worse, it has seemed to work, and the younger recruits claim that it "gives them strength." Some of the new officers say they are buoyed by the knowledge that their "heroes are alongside them," and that they will happily follow them into battle. "Our rank is less important that our experience," added a second lieutenant, being saluted by colonels.

This unique trend personifies a deeply ingrained Kurdish tradition—that of deep familial respect. In each unit under General Abdullah, one retired soldier is assigned to ten younger ones, and Sherdyl Rwandzi, forty-nine years old, is one of these. A taxi driver living in Bournmouth, England, he moved back to Kurdistan six months ago at the urging of his wife and stepmother, so he could join the "battle for humanity." His wife said to him, "If you don't fight for your country, then the foreigners will take it—and what will your children have left?" Following this, despite years of inaction, he called his old friend General Abdullah, and was handed a senior position.

This culture is in stark contrast with ISIS forces, who, despite their brutality (rumors of eighty more decapitations were spreading on Friday) are known also for their meritocracy. Simply put, the best fighters rise to the top, whereas, Kurdistan has always been plagued by nepotism. With US support that must surely change.

Kurdish Future

2014 was an incredibly difficult year for the Kurdish Regional Government in Iraq. A trilateral deal between Baghdad, KRG, and Turkey to use existing Turkish pipelines to sell Kurdish oil north had fallen through, and Baghdad had ceased to give them any of the national budget money it was supposed to (seventeen percent of all revenue).

The KRG needs around $750 million a month to pay its vast public sector, so when the Iraqi money was withheld pending resolution of the oil deals, the KRG was saddled with a growing amount of debt every month. On top of this, ISIS attacked in June, which forced the

Kurds to increase spending in order to deploy and supply troops. On top of this, they had to deal with 1.5 million refugees (about twenty percent of their current population).

So, looking ahead, the KRG must now use the opportunity ISIS has given it to strike deals for its long-term survival. First, they need a permanent deal with Turkey, to supply not just oil, but also gas for the next few decades. Second, they need a long-term security agreement with the United States, which will allow them to buy their own weapons without relying on the Baghdad government.

And it does seem as if they've got a great bargaining chip. They sit at the very heart of the Middle East, an area where the United States desperately needs allies it can count on. They are Westernized, friendly, they border Syria, Turkey, Iran, and Iraq, and are crying out to become the West's crucial allies in the coming decade. In September 2014, a delegation went to Washington to propose and outline such a security arrangement. It remains to be seen if the United States will agree to one.

A teenage boy filming clashes in Aleppo runs from sniper fire.

CHAPTER TWENTY-SIX

Social Media

Never before has a terrorist organization harnessed the power of social media the way ISIS has. Their ability to project their desired image is staggering, and is considered, alongside their military gains, to be their most dangerous tool. Twitter, YouTube, Facebook, Instagram, and Tumblr have become the core mode of communication and dissemination for their ideas, while also giving us valuable insights into their twisted world. Everything from the rhetoric used in posts, to clothing worn in videos, to music, to camera angles, is finely tuned, and serves three main aims: to recruit, to provoke, and to terrify—all have been successful.

The videos showing the beheadings of Western journalists and aid workers have been seared into the minds of the world's population, and by affecting public opinion, played a major part in Obama's decision to enter the fray. One cannot help but think that this provocation of the worst kind was done for precisely that reason, for the sight of Western planes dropping bombs in Syria serves their recruitment goals. At the same time, it should not have taken these videos to spur Obama into action; ISIS should have been targeted far earlier.

The videos showing the massacre of countless soldiers, which ISIS shares regularly, serve to sow fear among their enemies. When the thirty thousand Iraqi soldiers fled in the face of the ISIS attack, many did so out of the fear of meeting the same end. They knew they would not just be killed, they would be tortured and beheaded. Amazingly, despite the horror of the massacres, some of the videos have been edited to appear even more brutal.

Not only does ISIS have established media divisions and highly trained editors, but they also use sophisticated methods to extend their reach. Their Arabic language Twitter app "Dawn of Glad Tiding" allows members to flood the site with thousands of new "re-tweets" so they automatically start trending. ISIS hajacks current hash-tags, such as #brazil2014 or #france during the World Cup, so anybody searching for these innocuous events is accidentally exposed to ISIS propaganda.

Pro-ISIS clerics around the world help disseminate this content to a huge number of people. An extremist cleric like the Saudi, Muhammad al-Arifi, who was banned last year from the European Union for advocating wife-beating and hatred of Jews, commands a following of 9.4 million followers on Twitter. That's 9.4 million people subjected to his extremists views, and encouraged to support ISIS.

But before their content reaches the web, it is

compiled by a vast army of media workers and cameramen. According to a shopkeeper in Raqqa, the demand for high-definition video cameras is so great that it has led to a shortage in the city; on one occasion, this shopkeeper was asked to buy thirty cameras for one battalion, which he had delivered from Turkey. ISIS offers training for their media wings, and uses drones, multi camera edits, and highly advanced editing techniques.

Background

The idea of these media centers was born out of the Arab Spring, and played a large part in the overthrowing of President Ben Ali in Tunisia, Qaddafi in Libya, and Mubarak in Egypt, but it was in Syria where they became so well organized. As the Syrian conflict got worse, each city in rebel hands set up a media center—these were the first ports of call for journalists covering the brutal battles in Aleppo, Homs, Idlib, and other cities. As the war grew more dangerous, Western media companies started relying on these groups exclusively for their footage, provoking accusations that the world's media was encouraging young Syrians to put themselves in harm's way for coverage—without offering them any safety net, or even payment.

The reliance on videos off the Internet also resulted in a number of mistakes by major networks. For example, CNN broadcast footage of a young girl being pulled from rubble, which it turned out had actually been filmed years earlier in Kosovo. The sheer volume of clips emerging from the battlefield was immense, and in turn the potential for propaganda was huge.

Initially, many teenagers filmed battles for the rebels, in some cases those too young to fight were given cameras. Rick and I followed some of these "media kids" in Aleppo in 2012, young boys around fourteen, whose role was to sneak into Assad controlled areas of Aleppo and gather intel or film troop buildups. They were also tasked with filming the rebels as they fought and distributing it to other outlets. With tight jeans and slicked back hair, these guys belonged in a boy band, not in a war zone—they were fearless. One day, as Syrian rebels attempted to attack a regime post, I remember one of the boys jumping in front of the fighters, allowing them to fire over his head, so that he could get the best shot. Many of such media kids had been shot or caught in blasts themselves, a few had been caught by Assad's regime and tortured, and some had been killed. They were some of the bravest people I met, trying to show the world what was happening.

After a few more trips, I could see this becoming more organized, and each battalion had one or two fighters filming every minute of combat. These would be compiled and send to a hub, from where they would be edited, both for online Western media, and also for Syrian TV. There were a few rebel channels that would broadcast twenty-four hour footage from the battlefield to rousing Islamic music, and as the only form of entertainment at night, we would often sit around in the dark watching montages from the various battles that week, or various suicide attacks, as the people around us cried out "Allahu Akbar" whenever a decisive clip was shown.

Like everything else in the conflict, this was adopted, and perfected by ISIS. Today, their media wing is in overdrive, operating on so many different fronts. One sickening tool they use is the mock current affairs program that they force captured British journalist John Cantlie to host. On the show, he speaks directly to the camera, bringing the viewer up-to-date on specific battles, quoting foreign newspapers, and debunking Western news reports. When Western media claimed that Kurdish forces had captured the town of Kobane, Cantlie did a report from inside, talking to the camera in the style of any major broadcaster. The words, fluid and slick, ending with the sign off "Join me for the next program."

ISIS's propaganda message to potential recruits revolves around the creation of the caliphate. It highlights the evil done by Shia and foreign enemies, incites hatred and revenge, and basks in the glory that they will feel by restoring true word to the Sunni Martyrs. It has to be said that as far as foot soldiers go, this can be tempting, yet, there's no doubt that the leaders of ISIS have their own goals and power struggles which go as far as dealing with the Allawite "devils."

Dabiq

Dabiq is the printed magazine that ISIS produces— well edited, with slick publishing, and translated into various languages. Its main purpose is to ensure that ISIS's religious pedigree is strong, and so page after page drones on about its justifications and the sins of the infidels. It regularly mentions its political institutions, and its rule of law as it seek to explain itself. Ultimately, if ISIS is to compete with the older established jihadi networks, it needs to prove its own legitimacy, and Dabiq does this for the international market.

Dabiq, which is the name of a town in northern Syria where the Muslims and "Rome" are supposed to clash in their final showdown, is of huge significance to ISIS, and many of the articles, picture stories, and interviews featured within Dabiq refer to the final clash, which they believe is coming. The front covers of Dabiq often show Western icons —St. Peter's Square in the Vatican, US soldiers carrying their wounded, or Noah's ark.

Religious Propaganda

Compared with Osama bin Laden's blurry, crackly tapes, released from his mountain hideout and sent over land via donkey to the offices of Al Jazeera, Baghdadi's first TV appearance couldn't have been more different. In plain sight, he delivered a rousing sermon to the people of Mosul on July 4, 2014 in the Great Mosque of al-Nouri. Filmed by five high-definition cameras, inside and outside the mosque, it was a staged piece of theater. He wore the traditional clothes of the caliph, and a black turban to mimic what Mohammed was said to have worn on his conquest of Mecca. He quoted specific chapters of the Koran to focus on his own religious duty, spoke flawless classical Arabic, and carried a thin wooden rod, of the kind their Prophet Mohammed was known to carry.

Every small detail was geared toward showing his followers that they could take on the West and establish the caliphate, and the outcome was a finely tuned twenty-one minute video. Baghdadi has not been seen since, though he has released some audiotapes.

Social Media

For the foreign fighters in ISIS, social media has played a larger role than in any conflicts before it. More so than the official channels described above, social media is the real source of information and inspiration, and videos from inside ISIS territory show huge queues around the Internet cafes, which still operate under strict supervision. One such video shows a room full of ladies, dressed head to toe in the Niqab, all talking in French to their mothers and families back home. One of the women can be heard justifying her life under ISIS to her mother, saying, "I am happy here—I won't come back."

ISIS have a few core outlets to entice Western fighters, all made in the "Al Hayat Media Center." Their logo looks remarkably like Al Jazeera's, an attempt to give them legitimacy. Al Hayat is the foreign language channel that makes shows in German, English, and French. The videos are aimed at showing just how welcoming and wonderful ISIS can be. In one named "Eid Greetings," fighters from various countries speak about how rewarded and content they are to be there, openly asking their "brothers" to join them. "I don't think there's anything better than living in the land of Khalifa," says one fighter from the United Kingdom.

In the series entitled Mujatweets, a variety of short clips shows the pleasant side of fighting with ISIS. We see ISIS handing out candy floss to children, a German fighter singing in a lulling tone with a big smile on his face, and children playing with guns, and at a fairground. We are also told that those who join the battle may be so lucky as to smell of musk.

But images and graphic videos of murder also appeal to some of the recruits. The most violent and bloodthirsty among the foreign fighters are the ones who publish images of themselves online, standing proudly over dismembered bodies. There is the case of Abdel Bary from the United Kingdom, who boasted about his adventures in Syria on Twitter, posting a photo of himself holding a severed head in one hand with the caption, "'Chillin' with my homie, or what's left of him."

The use of social media by foreign fighters is just as important a propaganda tool as the slick edits released by the media arm. Every foreign fighter shares pictures and videos of themselves, not just killing, but supposedly living well, eating well, and enjoying the carnage. As a recruiting tool, this is powerful—it allows them to show all aspiring jihadists that the people out there are like them; that if they can do it, others can too. Reyaad Khan, a twenty-year-old from Portsmouth, England, shared pictures of a table covered in stews and rice with the caption: "While the U.S. think they are causing havoc and damage to ISIS, we kick back & keep moving. #ISIS"

Another taunts the West with images of him at a supermarket buying Nutella, saying, "I was so terrified by the U.S. air strikes I had to buy myself Nutella to comfort my brittle heart." To see how far into the social media world some of the fighters have come, we need only look at the writing of Khadijah Dare, a twenty-two-year-old British woman living in Syria with her husband, who used modern shorthand for her tweet, saying, "UK must b shaking up ha ha, I wna b da 1st UK woman 2 kill a UK or US terrorist!"

There is a concerted effort to remove official ISIS Twitter accounts or YouTube videos that show brutality, but just as fast as they are removed, new ones spring up and spread rapidly among the terrorist network for others to follow. Disseminating their message has never been so easy.

ISIS has begun to allow journalists to work under their rule—but this is farce. Below are rules to be followed in their censored world:

Journalists' Rules:

1. Correspondents must swear allegiance to the Caliph [Abu Bakr] al-Baghdadi ... they are subjects of the Islamic State and, as subjects, they are obliged to swear loyalty to their imam.

2. Their work will be under the exclusive supervision of the [ISIS] media offices.

3. Journalists can work directly with international news agencies (such as Reuters, AFP and AP), but they are to avoid all international and local satellite TV channels. They are forbidden to provide any exclusive material or have any contact (sound or image) with them in any capacity.

4. Journalists are forbidden to work in any way with the TV channels placed on the blacklist of channels that fight against Islamic countries (such as Al-Arabiya, Al Jazeera, and Orient). Violators will be held accountable.

5. Journalists are allowed to cover events in the governorate with either written or still images without having to refer back to the [ISIS] media office. All published pieces and photos must carry the journalist's and photographer's names.

6. Journalists are not allowed to publish any reportage (print or broadcast) without referring to the [ISIS] media office first.

7. Journalists may have their own social media accounts and blogs to disseminate news and pictures. However, the ISIS media office must have the addresses and name handles of these accounts and pages.

8. Journalists must abide by the regulations when taking photos within [ISIS territory] and avoid filming

locations or security events where taking pictures is prohibited.

9. ISIS media offices will follow up on the work of local journalists within [ISIS territory] and in the state media. Any violation of the rules in place will lead to suspending the journalist from his work, and he will be held accountable.

10. The rules are not final and are subject to change at any time depending on the circumstances and the degree of cooperation between journalists and their commitment to their brothers in the ISIS media offices.

11. Journalists are given a license to practice their work after submitting a license request at the [ISIS] media office.

CHAPTER TWENTY-SEVEN

Other Support for ISIS

ISIS has been attempting to spread its tentacles far and wide. Not only by encouraging lone wolf attacks around the world, but also by seeking alliances with other jihadi movements. They have sought discussions with leaders of other radical groups and have sent emissaries to a wide number of countries including Pakistan, Egypt, and Libya, with the intention of expanding.

They have had some success, namely among smaller groups looking to boost their own exposure, but none of their main international rivals (other Al-Qaeda franchises or Taliban groups) have yet heeded the call, or even acknowledged their right to be a Caliphate. The main thing to remember is that for them to successfully export their "caliphate" abroad, and to replicate their success, they would need the same perfect conditions that existed in Syria and Iraq. Namely massive destabilization within a failed (Islamic) state, resources they can control and profit from, avenues through which to sell those resources, and weapons caches they could seize and arm themselves with. Without those conditions, they will only ever be terrorist cells, not so-called states.

There are very few places in the world that are this troubled, but there is one country that fits the bill, offering all of these conditions: Libya. Libya is without a doubt a failed state, and various Islamist groups have already taken much of the country. Nobody is really in charge, the country is controlled by militias, and the national government has had to flee from the capital of Tripoli. With the capital now overrun with Islamic militants, the government has set up in the relative safety of Tobruk, a small coastal town, leaving militants to run amok elsewhere.

Like Syria and Iraq, Libya has huge oil reserves and vast land and sea borders from where it can be shipped or smuggled. Already we are seeing these resources taken over, not by ISIS, but certainly by other Islamic militants. There are countless weapons caches leftover from Qaddafi's era, as well as many tons of weapons sent by Gulf and Arab states to support the revolution in 2011 (Qatar stands out as the main supplier). Above all, there is the will of a widely extremist population, who are increasingly upset at the daily chaos and lack of rule.

These are exactly the conditions that allowed ISIS to thrive in Syria, and indeed ISIS already has control of its first Libyan city—Derna, a town of 150,000 on the eastern border near Egypt. ISIS first appeared here in September 2014 when militants aligned with Al-Qaeda and the Islamic Maghreb swore allegiance to ISIS. Videos on YouTube show hundreds of fighters in the town square pledging allegiance to Baghdadi, as they flocked from other warring groups, principally the Islamic Youth Shura Council.

If it's possible to imagine, the Islamic Youth Shura council is as brutal as ISIS, and enjoys public decapitations and beatings in the city's football stadium. It is only a small movement at the moment, and there are still other jihadi factions who have not sworn allegiance to ISIS, but it is a terrible threat in a country just across from Europe. Many of the fighters joining ISIS in Libya are from other parts of Africa, again mirroring the buildup of extremists in Syria.

US General David Rodriguez, the commander of US troops in Africa, has also confirmed the presence of ISIS training camps in Libya: "ISIS has begun its efforts over in the east out there, to introduce some people. It's mainly about coming for training and logistics support right now. As far as a huge command and control network, I've not seen that yet."

We may not have seen it yet, but let us not forget how poorly the United States misread the situation on the ground back in 2012, which led to the murder of Ambassador Christopher Stevens and three other Americans. With this in mind, it's imperative that we don't allow the situation in Libya to get any worse.

Pakistan / Afghanistan

Pakistan and Afghanistan are prime targets for ISIS—not necessarily so they can expand their territory yet, but because these two countries are veritable breeding grounds for terrorists, and are considered the home of jihad. In many ways, if ISIS can establish themselves there, they can begin to rival Al-Qaeda in the global jihadi arena, and in turn have access to a huge pool of possible recruits.

As such, the same ideological battle that is going on between Islamists the world over is being keenly felt in Pakistan and Afghanistan. Young jihadists who have grown up looking to Al-Qaeda as their moral leaders are starting to consider ISIS as the true force—for only they have had made real gains. So what ISIS and Baghdadi have done is to directly address these areas, trying to persuade them that they are the only representatives of jihad.

There is certainly a large ideological following for ISIS within Pakistan and Afghanistan, and their flags appear around the country, in market places, streets, and bazaars. But they have not yet been able to wrest any real, practical control from traditional groups. This may change, but for the moment, very few Taliban leaders have come out in full favor of ISIS. This is because the jihadi situation in Pakistan and Afghanistan is very complicated and the long established factions within the Taliban play an intricate domestic game with each other and indeed with the government, making it very hard for ISIS to get a foothold. Some minor Taliban leaders have pledged allegiance to ISIS, and have established an affiliate Ansar-ul Daulat-e Islamia fil Pakistan, but at this point it is mainly useful for recruitment. With the United States pullout of Afghanistan, this may change.

Other Franchises

Just across the border from Libya, Egypt is also coming to terms with its two revolutions. When the Muslim Brotherhood government, led by Muhammed Morsi, was overthrown by General Sisi in 2013, Egypt went on the offensive against the extremists. However, the Brotherhood maintains a large following, and continues to thrive, mainly in Sinai. Ansar Beit al-Maqdis, a group happy to kill civilians and soldiers alike, have also sworn allegiance to ISIS. Not a lot is known about Ansar Beit al-Maqdis, who has only been around since 2011, but already they number up to a few thousand, and are said to include both foreigners and a large number of Bedouins.

Initially, they directed their violence against Israel, sending rockets across the border. But they have been expanding, and now attack inside Cairo, as well as Jordanian oil pipelines, and frequently plant roadside bombs around the east of the country. Born out of the first Egyptian revolution, they have tweeted that there was "no use to continue with shameful peace or blasphemous democracy."

In Algeria, Jund al-Khalifa, once part of Al-Qaeda in the Islamic Maghrab, have joined ISIS, claiming that Al-Qaeda has "deviated from the true path," while in other parts of the world, from the Philippines to Indonesia, small groups have also pledged allegiance, though really only in name Yahya.

CHAPTER TWENTY-EIGHT

What Lies Ahead

In a refugee camp in Turkey I saw a drawing by a girl of thirteen which showed bodies lying in graves; their arms and legs in a pile. Next to it she had drawn heads standing on walls and tanks firing on flowers. Under it she had written, "There was a beautiful country Syria that was taken by evil, and now our people are tortured." Another image said simply, "I pity my country, I pity my life."

The Syrian War, the Assad regime, and ISIS have together displaced millions of families, and this mass migration of people has been one of the most devastating effects of the conflict. Countries are overflowing with men, women, and children, and each has a tale of brutality and misery to tell. For many it will define them forever—and for the children there is little hope.

The camps in which they live can be horrific. In the summer months, their tents become saunas, and in the winter they barely stave off the cold. Rain, snow, and mud seeps into them and, in some camps, clogs the rudimentary sewage systems; human waste runs amid the tents. Children who have grown up knowing nothing else play in this mud, while the old, sit vacantly looking out; resigned.

I cannot exaggerate the scale of this—and whatever images you may have seen cannot convey the magnitude. It is an exodus of people unlike any we've seen since the Second World War, and the numbers are growing.

In some camps there are 150 people for each bathroom, and fifteen families to a tent. Food is delivered sporadically, and water barely clean. It's hard to imagine how so many get by, with so little but they do, and what strikes you as you walk around is their resilience.

People who have lost everything—possessions, homes, relatives, countries—show incredible fortitude. They have so little, but they give so much, and it's impossible to go to a camp and not be invited in for tea by everyone you stop. They are willing to share their last piece of bread, their last plate of food, and they do so with a smile on their face. Grateful that people came, that people remembered, and that they're alive. Everyone will tell you that someone, somewhere is worse off than they are.

Countless families carry pictures of those they've lost, those who have gone back to fight, or those they can't find, but most tragically is that many have little hope in sight. They live in a purgatory, with nothing to pass the time except their thoughts.

In January 2015 twelve million people had been forced to leave their homes with nothing, forced to seek out an existence somewhere else. That is half the total population of Syria—half of the whole country, and many of them are children. 1.2 million lost in Lebanon, 1.6 million in Turkey, six hundred thousand in Jordan, three hundred thousand in Iraq, the list goes on—and these countries are feeling the strain.

I met a boy of ten years old who refused to play with others, repeatedly telling teachers, "I am a man, give me a gun, I want to fight," and I met another at the age of twelve who wanted ISIS bodies to burn, like they had burnt his brothers. He showed no remorse, and wanted to kill. I firmly believe that more must be done to rid the world of ISIS. They are creating a generation of disease, and if we stand any chance of helping, we have to act. As I have said throughout—inaction is not an option.

CHAPTER TWENTY-NINE

Conclusion

Ever since I started writing this book, I've been think-ing about its conclusion. But now that I'm here, it's hard to know what to say. The horror, the brutality, and the violence are one thing, while the geopolitical issues and military options on the ground are altogether different.

I understand that for each possible solution there are a hundred possible problems. And that among a hundred possible outcomes, there may be no solution at all. Nevertheless, if we don't strive for an answer we won't find one, and inaction is the worst possible path.

There is one great problem with foreign policy, and that is that it's often only based around a four (or five) year electoral cycle. But if we're to effect any real change overseas, we have to think in the fifty or one hundred year cycle—there are simply no quick solutions. Foreign policies which encourage education, the separation of church and state, and democracy are crucial, but so is the realization that centralized governments may not work in many tribal countries, and we must look at ways to develop federalization when other differences can't be overcome.

1. Obama's Strategy

Militarily ISIS will eventually wither—but it will take years, and the seeds will be sown for future generations of conflicts. General Allen has laid out the path to follow and it's sixfold: "A military campaign, disrupting the flow of foreign fighters, counter finance, humanitarian relief and ideological delegitimization." All very valid, but this will take too long, and during that time ISIS will have planted roots, brainwashed its children, and wasted its lands. More must be done and sooner.

Obama's policy seems to be one of counter-terrorism. It doesn't appear as if he has a long-term solution, but instead seeks to contain ISIS and degrade their strength, while hoping that something good will come of it. However without dealing with the underlying problems, the situation will just continue to simmer, and sooner or later we will face it all again.

Ultimately, Obama's laissez-faire attitude suggests that it's the regional powers' problem to deal with, not his. But I don't believe this—it is our problem, and to rely on the regional powers to shape the Middle East won't work. Two of history's great enemies, Saudi Arabia and Iran (Sunni and Shia) simply won't stop until they've burnt each other out, and millions will die in the ensuing battle. We can't sit by as that happens—not least because it would have repercussions the world over.

Dropping bombs can't dislodge ISIS either. It can stop them taking territory, but it can't root them out; and to do that we need Special Forces. We must be willing to commit limited troops on the ground and not be ashamed of it; we need these alongside regional allies such as the Kurds, Jordanians, FSA, and some Sunni tribes.

Obama insists that Assad and ISIS must go—but he's done nothing decisive about either. If he was serious about it, he would be supporting opposition groups to fill the vacuum, but he hasn't—on the contrary, he walked away from them.

Moving forward, the United States must absolutely continue training and supplying vetted opposition groups on the fringes of Syria, or it will have no say in the future of the region. To call for the removal of Assad and ISIS without offering a replacement, is a dead end policy.

A senior military source told me that the Obama administration has begun seriously reconsidering their Syrian strategy, as they have started to realize that Assad must go before they can defeat ISIS. Apparently everyone from Kerry down is moving in this direction, but Obama alone won't budge.

While much significance is put on Iran supporting Assad, I believe that US intervention would force the Iranians to push Assad out. They are too pragmatic to support Assad in the face of a real US campaign, and in turn would seek a diplomatic solution—one which would see Assad leave power, and see his replacement federalize the country.

2. *A Federal Iraq*

It appears likely that Iraq (supported by coalition troops) will successfully destroy ISIS on the battlefield—and indeed it's happening already. Iraqi troops (backed by others) are slowly taking back the western province of Anbar, and Kurdish troops are moving towards the northern city of Mosul. This won't happen quickly, (particularly in the cities), nor will it happen without Western support on the ground, but it will happen in the coming years.

Just because ISIS is defeated in Iraq however doesn't mean that peace will last. There are still immense sectarian divisions to overcome before this can happen, and for there to be a positive future in the country, I believe a federal system must be adopted; one which splits the country in three zones; Sunni, Shia, and Kurdish.

3. *Remove Assad, Work with Turkey*

The Syrian conflict, and the chaos that ensued, are a direct product of President Assad's brutality, and while we hear figures of thirty odd thousand ISIS fighters on the battlefield, this is nothing compared with the seventeen odd million residents of Syria who do not support them.

It's my firm belief that the future of Syria is in the hands of these citizens, those who are tired of war and sick of fighting, and have nothing to do with the brutality of ISIS. If we are to empower them, and encourage them to rise up, there is only one option—Assad must be removed. Remove Assad, and people have no reason to continue their tactical alliance with rebel groups.

The other benefit of removing of Assad is that Turkey would join the battle. Turkey, despite their reluctance to help so far, is in fact very much on our side in this conflict, they just see no benefit to themselves unless Assad is removed first. Remove Assad, and Turkey joins in, closes its border to jihadists, prevents their oil from being sold. The United States could use its bases in the region, and Turkey might even join the coalition as an active partner. There is talk of a safe zone along their border where refugees could move, but that's a long way off.

The other major role Turkey could play would be in supporting a no-fly zone. Ultimately Assad's ability to project power is reliant on his air force and despite talk of his advanced Russian made air defense systems, officials assure me this would pose no problem to coalitions jets. Assad would soon be grounded, and his power would wane.

4. Religious Reformation

ISIS is not an army—it's an ideology—so how can we hope to destroy it? On one level, I have to say we will never really defeat ISIS (or at least radical Islam)—not in our lifetimes. It feeds on destruction, including its own, so the weaker it gets, the more hardened its core becomes. There will always be fanatics hoping to thrive off the misery of others.

And of course, we will always have the fifteen thousand angry jihadists, the true believers of ISIS who are never going to change. Even if they surrender, they aren't going to repent, and they'll disappear into the shadows to try again one day. It's likely that this threat will always be there lingering.

But is it too much to imagine that the Middle East might go through a reformation in the same way that Europe did in the sixteenth and seventeenth centuries? Ultimately, ISIS is driven by fervent Islam, but through their brutality, they have to erode its power. Many Muslims have said that ISIS is hugely damaging to the future of Islam, and that, eventually, it will result in a backlash against it. I know that reformation would take a long time too—but it happened in Europe following the inquisition of the 1520's, following the brutal persecution of counselmen in the name of religion. The corruption and erosion of the papacy (in this case the spiritual leaders of jihad), the rise of nationalism and the learning of the Renaissance are all events we must try to replicate.

Perhaps everything we're seeing in the Middle East is merely the region coming to terms with progress, as it hauls itself slowly into the modern era. But perhaps it's the opposite, and the region is sinking ever further into the past. For the sake of millions of lives, lets hope it's the former.

EPILOGUE

Sinjar

Ranir, 35, buried her daughter with her own hands and the help of a stranger. It was September, and the ground was easy to dig. She had taken her body from the hospital, and dug a hole before leaving her in peace, swaddled in sheets and covered in stones.

For days she scoured the mountain with pictures of them, asking each of the fleeing families, "Have you seen this man, have you seen this woman." Nobody could help. She was alone, desperate, and ready to die.

A day earlier they'd been at home in northern Iraq when an ISIS shell landed on the house. A barrel of oil outside had been hit, and the explosion had sent shrapnel into her daughters side leaving her badly wounded. She was just twenty. Ranir had rushed her to the hospital trying to stem the bleeding, while all the time, more mortars rained down.

When they got there she was met with a scene of chaos—people bleeding on the floors, trying to get help, and only a few doctors still there. But they were lucky and her daughter was taken into a room, hooked up to a rare blood bag, and the medical staff began to patch her up. That was when ISIS arrived.

They entered the hospital with guns—shooting the men and wounded on the floors, rampaging thorough-out and carrying their own fighters in need of medical help. Ranir heard them come, but had nowhere to go—her daughter was unable to move.

When ISIS burst in the door Ranir tried to stop them; she pushed them away and begged them to show mercy, but they knocked her away, pulled out the tubes, rolled her daughter off the table, and dumped her on the floor. That was where she died, bleeding to death in her mother's arms while the men forced the doctor by gunpoint to help their own man.

Sometime later, when the men had left she emerged. There were bodies and blood covering the corridors, and people were moving and crawling around wounded. She tried to carry her daughter's body but couldn't, until someone saw her and helped. They drove to her house and buried her there and then she was alone. She wandered around for a while before eventually joining the exodus and walking to Mount Sinjar. When I spoke to her she said her life has been taken by ISIS.

She wishes now that she had been killed—how she wished they'd been gassed like the Kurds, how she wished that she hadn't been alive to see this pain. She hopes that someone will come and stop them, that someone will come to help her and others, that someone will give them back their lives, but she doesn't think anyone will.

If anyone has a doubt that ISIS needs to be destroyed or that we need to help do it, listen to people like Ranir.

They've had everything taken, and they're crying out for help.

APPENDIX

Al-Madina Treatise

All praises are to Allah, the Champion of the believers and Defeater of the criminals. Peace and prayers be on the Imam of the mujahideen, leader of the resplendent, and on his family and companions, protectors of the community of believers and of the clear truth, and whoever follows them until the Day of Judgment.

We congratulate the Islamic ummah [nation] in general and the lions of the Islamic State of Iraq and Syria on Allah's clear victory that He bestowed on his servants, the mujahideen. Here is the Islamic State accepting its victories with the grace of Allah, which is the sought-after caliphate and its legitimate course.

Thanks to Allah, its trunk is strengthened and its space is expanding. It knows no regression or retreat, no acquiescence or bowing down. Its sole purpose it to establish the sovereignty of Allah on earth, pave the way for enacting shari'a [Islamic law], and sweep away the law of the jungle from the land of Muslims.

We offer these short and sweet lines to our genuine clans, our families, and loved ones in the blessed State of Ninwa:

1. We bring you and Islamic world good tidings of these holy victories and of freeing prisoners from the prisons of the tyrannical Rafidi [rejecters, meaning the Shi'a] apostates, at the hands of your valiant sons of the Islamic State and its soldiers who sacrificed their own lives in order to smash their brothers' chains and release the ropes from them. Thousands of their imprisoned brothers were set free. They also conquered Badoush Fortress, the Police Directorate Prison, Al-Mukafaha Prison, and Tasfirat Prison with firm, confident hearts and strong resolve, breaking the necks of their enemies, rubbing the tyrants' noses on the prisons' steps, crushing the arrogance of the Safavids with the feet of the Victors.

2. It is all right for someone to ask: Who are you? The answer is: We are the soldiers of the Islamic State of Iraq and Syria, who have, from the roots of Islam, we have taken it upon ourselves to reinstate the glorious Islamic caliphate, push oppression and injustice away from our people and brothers after the Safavid snake had coiled around the necks of the Muslims, and worked to chop off its head and release the coils.

3. We treat people according to what they reveal and what is inside of them we leave up to Allah. The original nature of mankind is Islam. We do not judge people by our own suspicions, rather by unequivocal evidence and gleaming proof. We give precedence to giving the benefit of the doubt towards any Muslim unless they are spies for attackers or accomplices to criminals.

4. People under our rule will be safe and comforted. By Allah, there can be no prosperity without Islamic rule to guarantee its citizens' rights and do justice to the oppressed whose rights were suppressed. Those who were yesterday discontented with us are now safe citizens, except for those who repel, denounce, or reject the faith.

5. The wealth that was in the hands of the Safavid government (public funds) will be the responsibility of the Imam of the Muslims. He will dispose of it to the benefit of the Muslims, not to anyone who lays his hands on it, looting and plundering, or any action of the sort. If he does so, he exposes himself to legal action and accountability before the law followed by a deterrent punishment. The same applies to the protection of private possessions such as money, furnishings, and belongings from the theft of such assets, on the condition they are worth no less than the minimum liable amount of wealth and indisputably belong to the claimant. Such theft will be punished by cutting off of the hand. We will deal with armed robbery gangs as corrupters of the land and will invoke on them the words of our Lord, Most High: << Indeed,

the penalty for those who wage war against Allah and His Messenger and strive upon earth [to cause] corruption is none but that they be killed or crucified or that their hands and feet be cut off from opposite sides or that they be exiled from the land. That is for them a disgrace in this world; and for them in the Hereafter is a great punishment. >> (Al-Ma'idah: 33). Whosoever terrorizes Muslims with threats and extortion will be dealt the harshest of deterrent punishments if so proven against him.

6. Masajid [Mosques] are the houses of Allah: the ultimate of goals, the soul of all pastures, the pinnacle of all sanctuaries, maintained by the prayer-goers and infused with goodness and gratitude, people of the Adnani messenger {Prophet Muhammad]. [Our] blood and souls, selves and treasures mean nothing compared to the value of masajid. We entreat all Muslims to perform the prayers at their appointed times in congregation, applying the hadith (saying) of the Prophet, peace be upon him, "Prayer in congregation is better than twenty-five prayers of a man alone."

7. Our scholars, our strong tribal shaykhs, and our preachers are the crowns [of our people] and delight of our souls: Come together to an honorable stance to which history hearkens, and from which the face of eternity dawns. Come to a serious, honest stance to fend off the aggression of the poisonous Rafidis. Come to Islamic kinship in the melting pot of jihad and to a steady stream of support. Let us be as one solid row,

the way our Lord loves and orders us to go in one pioneering procession.

8. Beware, beware of dealing with agents [of foreign powers] and courting the government. The path is clear and the way of unbelief has been unmasked. We now act in the present, and the repentant from sin is as if he has no sins. Now forbidden is the trading and abuse of alcohol, drugs, and smoking, and all other forbidden acts.

9. As for the apostates among the army, police, and all other unbelieving apparatuses, the door to repentance is open to whoever wishes. We have designated places to receive the repenters in accordance with certain rules and conditions. As for he who persists and holds to his apostasy, his fate is none other than death, according to the hadith of the Prophet, peace be upon him, "Whoever replaces his religion, kill him."

10. As for councils, associations, and banners of all titles, and bearing arms, we do not accept these at all, in application of the words of the Prophet, "Whosoever comes to you while you are together as one entity, wishing to disrupt your solidarity or divide your community, kill him." Reported by Muslim. In another narration by Muslim, "Strike him with the sword whoever it may be."

11. Allah, Most High, has ordered togetherness and partnership and rejection of disparity and conflict. The troubles of the

group are better than the serenity of disparity. Division is the snare of Satan. The fragmentation of Muslims is a source of weakness. In alliances under the banner of pure, genuine faith is found much goodness. Too many ideologies and whims instigate bigotry and haughtiness which diminishes the blessings and pleasure of jihad. And Allah is the One whose help is sought. When Allah empowers his good servants who strive on His path, they lay the way for the dominance of shari'a, rule justly and fairly, and ease the burdens on people's shoulders caused by putrid, man-made laws. Performing one rule of Allah on earth is better for humanity than forty days of rain.

12. Our stance towards polytheist monuments and tombs and idolatrous shrines is manifested in the authentic instruction of the Prophet, peace be upon him, "Do not leave one idol standing without obliterating it, and do not leave an arrogant tomb without flattening it."

13. To the virtuous and honorable women: Allah calls you to modesty, chastity, and loose-fitting gowns. Settling at home and staying in an honorable room, avoiding going out unless out of necessity, this is the way of the Mothers of the Believers and the dignified women Companions, may Allah be pleased with them all.

14. Enjoy and be blessed under the balanced and gentle Islamic rule in a land where Muslims are the leaders, victors, rulers, and legislators.

15. In conclusion, we decorate the preamble of this treatise and say: Oh, People, you have experienced all secular systems, and have seen the eras of kings, republics, Baathists, and Safavids. You have tried them all, have tasted their bitterness and been burnt by their flames. Here we are now in the era of the Islamic State and the age of Imam Abi Bakr Al-Qurashi. You will see, with Allah's strength and success, the extent of the wide difference between an oppressive secular government that exhausts people's energies, muzzles their mouths, and violates their rights and dignities, and between a Qurashi imamate that takes revelation as its approach, with its clear and pure justice, where leadership accepts the advice of the great and the ordinary, the free and the slave, with no difference between light and dark skins. We establish justice upon ourselves before others as our Lord Almighty has said, << O you who have believed, be persistently standing firm in justice, witnesses for Allah, even if it be against yourselves or parents and relatives. Whether one is rich or poor, Allah is more worthy of both. So follow not ... >> (A-Nisaa: 135) Our intention is for the sake of Allah.

Islamic State of Iraq and Syria

Media Bureau of the State of Nineveh

ACKNOWLEDGMENTS

I'd like to thank Rick Findler, whom I trust with my life, and without whom this adventure would not have happened. I'd like to thank everyone who has made my journeys through the Middle East possible and kept me alive. Zaher Said, who has been our guide through some of the darkest places. Rizgar Saeed, our oldest friend in Iraq. Shwan Ali at the Palace Hotel in Sulemaniyah—a home from home. Deroy Murdock, who encouraged me, believed in me, and set me on this path. My wonderful patient agent, Jennifer Cohen who arrived from nowhere and placed her faith in me. Alexandra Peer Watson, our meticulous copy editor.

To Bosco and Hackett.

Thank you all.

AUTHOR'S NOTE

It's so hard to accurately gauge the true figures of ISIS fighters, foreign fighters, how much money they're earning, or how many people they're killing. In writing this book I have read the few sources available on the subject—be it from think tanks, intelligence services, governmental papers, or ISIS propaganda, but I've done so only to cross check research from primary sources.

A number of existing resources I looked at differed greatly from one another, and as such, a few of the figures herein will not match with others. That being said, I've chosen to write this book based on interviews with those who have fought with ISIS, and those who have fought against them. Those who have funded them and those who have fled from them. I've spoke to distant academics and to local farmers, and somewhere in the middle lies the truth.

My aim, rather than to be analytical, is to take you inside ISIS—to show you where they're from, how they fight, and why they hate. There's no doubt that these figures and details will continue to change as we continue to analyze them and as the situation evolves.

Thanks to:

Brookings Institute

The International Institute for Strategic Studies

United States State Department

United States Treasury Department

www.9-11commission.gov/

The Soufan Group

www.Bellingcat.com

www.jihadology.net

The Clarion Project

Wikileaks

International Centre for Not for Profit Law

United States institute of Peace

Stratfor

www.understandingwar.com